D0324526

365 Pocket™ Evening Prayers

Comfort and Peace to End Each Day

DAVID R. VEERMAN

Tyndale House Publishers, Inc., Carol Stream, Illinois

Visit Tyndale online at www.tyndale.com.

TYNDALE, Tyndale's quill logo, and *LeatherLike* are registered trademarks of Tyndale House Publishers, Inc. *365 Pocket* is a trademark of Tyndale House Publishers, Inc.

365 Pocket Evening Prayers: Comfort and Peace to End Each Day

Designed by Erik M. Peterson

Produced in association with The Livingstone Corporation.

ISBN 978-1-4143-8355-2

Printed in China

19 18 17 16 15 14 13
7 6 5 4 3 2 1

INTRODUCTION

Prayer is simply talking with God. As people of faith, we can come to him anytime, approach him anywhere, and pray about anything. God loves our honest, heartfelt prayers, and he cares deeply about the details of our lives. Evening, when we tend to reflect on the triumphs and trials of the day just past, is a natural time to draw close to God. Through prayer, we can invite him into our internal conversation, whether to thank him for his goodness or to seek his perspective on unresolved concerns.

Perhaps your faith is relatively new and you're not yet comfortable praying. This book is for you. The prayers we've developed can be claimed as your own conversations with God. As you pray through each topic and day, we hope you will become more comfortable talking with God and will even begin to form your own prayers to him.

Perhaps you've been a believer for years but need a little inspiration in your prayer life. This book is for you, too. We all have times when we repeat the same prayers over and over. Because it includes a year's worth of unique prayers that cover a broad range of topics, this book can help rejuvenate your dialogue with God.

Thank God that we don't have to be spiritually mature or "on fire" to have a meaningful prayer life! Wherever you are in your spiritual journey, God delights when you draw near to him. We hope this little book will help you do so.

You will find 365 prayers, arranged by days and topics. You can pray through each day of the year consecutively if you wish. Alternatively, look in the index for a topic that will help you pray through an urgent need or give words to something you may be experiencing. Every few days you will also find prayers called *Prayerful Moments.* These are shorter prayers for days when time is limited or for when you need a quick word with God.

As you enter into a new prayer, take it slow. Spend some time thinking about what you're saying to God, and try to personalize each prayer for your own life. Making each written prayer your own honest praise or petition will make it more meaningful.

In your conversations with God, take some time to listen. Reading God's Word as a part of your prayer time gives the Lord an opportunity to speak to you, too. You won't want to miss what he has to say! We've included a Scripture verse at the end of each prayer to help you ponder what God might be communicating to you.

Thank you for joining us on this quest for a deeper prayer life. It is our hope that by the end of this book, you will be inspired in your conversations with God and—most important—feel closer to him than ever before. It is often in these special times of prayer that God does his powerful work in our hearts. So don't give up; stick with it. As his Word says to us, "Let us come boldly to the throne of our gracious God. There we will receive his mercy, and we will find grace to help us when we need it most" (Hebrews 4:16).

The privilege of prayer is that it ushers us straight into the presence of our loving God. And Scripture promises us that he won't disappoint! With that in mind, it's time to begin.

A prayer about BEING KNOWN
When I think about God's omniscience

MY AMAZING GOD,
Admitting this is difficult, but I confess that at times I feel anonymous, as though no one knows who I am or even cares. Some days I feel abandoned and alone, even in a crowd. And at other times, in stressful situations, I feel lost. At those occasions I need to remember the powerful affirmation by David in Psalm 139. Lord, you have always known me. You know everything about me—my entire history beginning at conception and continuing right through my future; my DNA; my gifts and abilities; my sins and shortcomings; my challenges, failures, and successes; my thoughts, desires, and dreams. And you always know where I have been, where I am, and where I will be. I am not lost but found. I am not abandoned but wanted. I am not anonymous. And as David says, "You go before me and follow me"—my ever-present ally and friend. Thank you, Father, for creating, loving, watching, guarding, and guiding me. I am known; I am loved; I am yours. And now I can sleep in peace, fully resting in you.

O LORD, you have examined my heart and know everything about me. You know when I sit down or stand up. You know my thoughts even when I'm far away. You see me when I travel and when I rest at home. You know everything I do. You know what I am going to say even before I say it, LORD. You go before me and follow me. You place your hand of blessing on my head. Such knowledge is too wonderful for me, too great for me to understand! PSALM 139:1-6

DAY 2

A prayer about TRUST IN OTHERS
When my cynicism shows

DEAR LORD,
I have been burned so often that I am finding it difficult to trust anyone. Today someone made a promise, and I thought, *Yeah, right—that'll never happen!* I don't want to be a cynical or skeptical person, Lord. Everyone is a sinner—no one's perfect, and I shouldn't expect them to be; eventually every relative, friend, neighbor, coworker, and others will let me down. I expect to be understood and forgiven when I fail to live up to something I said or when I fail and fall, and I should offer the same understanding and forgiveness to others. My lack of trust has hurt my relationships because I have been keeping my distance emotionally. I want to be a loving person, and you have told me that love "never loses faith." So when young people act their age, help me to cut them some slack. When imperfect and finite people act negatively, help me to see them as you do and forgive. And when I've been hurt repeatedly, give me strength to endure "through every circumstance." I want to trust again.

Love never gives up, never loses faith, is always hopeful, and endures through every circumstance.
1 CORINTHIANS 13:7

DAY 3

A prayer about JEALOUSY
When I begin to resent others for what they have

HOLY SPIRIT,

I have a strong drive to do my best and be the best I can be. That's fine, I know, but this tendency makes me susceptible to seeing others as competitors as I compare myself to them and what they have. And that can lead to jealousy. I see someone achieving a milestone, earning an award, attaining status and recognition, or receiving a wonderful gift, and I begin to resent him or her for having what I wish I had. Forgive me, Holy Spirit. I know that left unchecked, jealousy can eat me up, consume my thoughts, and bring me down. Yes, I need to strive to do well, but I also need to be content with how you have made me and the gifts and opportunities you have given me. Just because only one team can win the grand championship in a sport doesn't mean that the others are losers. Continue to show me when I'm having those jealous thoughts—do your convicting work in me. And give me the grace to sincerely celebrate with others in *their* successes.

Anger is cruel, and wrath is like a flood, but jealousy is even more dangerous. PROVERBS 27:4

A prayer about APPEARANCE
When I'm self-conscious about how I look

DEAR GOD,
I spent a lot of time today trying to look my best—the right clothes and every hair in place. I wanted to project the right image, make a good impression. I know I should take care of myself and that sloppiness is not next to godliness. But at times I think I'm way too concerned about my appearance, almost obsessed. In fact, I can hardly pass my reflection without checking myself out. Am I that insecure, Lord? Maybe I'm just overly influenced by a society that highly prizes physical beauty—perfect hair, skin, physique. Yet that cultural value isn't new and seems to have navigated the centuries, since you had to remind Samuel not to judge by outward appearance as he was searching for your man to lead Israel. Forgive me, Lord, for misplaced priorities, and help me focus on my inward beauty, my heart.

The LORD said to Samuel, "Don't judge by his appearance or height, for I have rejected him. The LORD doesn't see things the way you see them. People judge by outward appearance, but the LORD looks at the heart." 1 SAMUEL 16:7

A prayer about DEATH
When I consider my mortality

FATHER GOD,
Lately I have been reminded about the brevity of life—it goes so fast. I'm getting older, and I feel it. And when I hear about someone my age dying, I realize that it could have been me. I know death is inevitable, of course—everyone dies eventually, some much sooner than others—but usually I put that truth out of my mind; I just don't want to think about it . . . until something shocks me back to reality. I say that I don't fear death because I know I will live eternally with you. I do believe that and trust you fully for my salvation. But at times I'm afraid of the prospect of dying, of leaving all I hold dear on earth. Mostly, I fear the deaths of those I love, especially those who don't know you. Oh, how I wish they would give their lives to you and be assured of their eternal destiny. Please, God, calm my anxious heart and help me remember that you are always with me—here, in death, and beyond.

When our dying bodies have been transformed into bodies that will never die, this Scripture will be fulfilled: "Death is swallowed up in victory. O death, where is your victory? O death, where is your sting?"
1 CORINTHIANS 15:54-55

DAY 6 *Prayerful Moment*

A prayer about HOPE
When I begin to fear the worst

PRECIOUS SAVIOR,
Recently many of my great and grand plans disintegrated. I thought I had life figured out . . . but now not so much. I'm not sure which way to turn. So I'm depending on you, Jesus, trusting you fully. I know you have nothing but good planned for me. I hope in you alone.

"I know the plans I have for you," says the LORD. "They are plans for good and not for disaster, to give you a future and a hope." JEREMIAH 29:11

DAY 7 *Prayerful Moment*

A prayer about CARING FOR OTHERS
When I see someone in need

LORD JESUS,
I confess that I can become so focused on my own concerns that I look right past others. Yet every day I come in contact with hurting people—some suffering physically, others emotionally or financially; and so many who don't know you. Open my eyes, Lord, to the needs around me. Open my checkbook so that I will give generously. Open my schedule so I can spend time sharing the Good News. I want to see others the way you see them and to respond the way you would.

Don't just pretend to love others. Really love them.
ROMANS 12:9

A prayer about MEETING THE CHALLENGE
When I complain about my problems

DEAR LORD,

Jeremiah faced terrible opposition and conflict. Yet he faithfully served as your spokesperson to the people of Judah just before they were taken captive. After hearing of a plot to kill him, Jeremiah complained and asked why he had to endure so much while wicked people were prosperous and happy. I am convicted, Lord, when I read your response—that if those problems were tiring him, how would he ever be able to "race against horses"? My problems don't come close to what Jeremiah faced, yet I complain and often think in self-pity, *Why me?* Instead, I should see them as opportunities to develop my endurance so that I am ready for the challenges ahead. Nothing catches you by surprise, and nothing is impossible for you. So I am confident that with you I can persevere and overcome. Thank you for my troubles now and in the future. I know that you are allowing me to meet and work through them in order to prepare me for even greater challenges. I want to be able to race against horses.

If racing against mere men makes you tired, how will you race against horses? If you stumble and fall on open ground, what will you do in the thickets near the Jordan?
JEREMIAH 12:5

DAY 9

A prayer about FUTURE FEARS
When I am concerned about what lies ahead

FATHER GOD,

I remember the plaque on the wall that read, "I may not know what the future holds, but I know who holds the future." It's true! But I sometimes act as though it isn't, or I simply forget. You do, in fact, hold the future because you are all powerful and know everything; nothing happens outside of your knowledge and control. I also believe that you want the very best for me and are always with me. And looking back, I see how you have worked in my life. So why am I afraid of what *might* happen tomorrow or next month or next year or ten years from now? Even when I expect to face a difficult challenge—job interview, conflict-resolution session, awkward relationship, financial deadline, court date, or hospital operation—I should know that you will work out *everything* for my good and your glory. You have promised to do exactly that. Please calm my fears and help me hold on to the truth. I want to walk confidently into the future, one step, one day, at a time.

Remember the things I have done in the past. For I alone am God! I am God, and there is none like me. Only I can tell you the future before it even happens. Everything I plan will come to pass, for I do whatever I wish. ISAIAH 46:9-10

A prayer about REJECTION
When I feel put down

DEAR JESUS,
Recently friends turned their backs on me, and I feel terrible. I don't handle rejection very well. That includes an idea shot down, an application denied, a relationship broken, and other slights, real or imagined, big or small. Taking each rejection personally, I wonder what's wrong with me. My self-image and confidence are taking a hit. I need to recall how you deal with me, Savior. You don't reject me, but welcome me and pull me close. Although you don't always approve of what I do, you accept me as I am, a person made in your image and a sinner saved by grace. Further, you love me and called me to be God's very own child. You certainly know what I am experiencing because you were despised and rejected by the religious leaders of your day and the crowd, enduring their verbal insults and physical torture. You were abandoned by your closest friends, who ran for their lives. And you hung on the cross, alone, for me. Help me remember that I am yours, and that's enough.

They will do all this to you because of me, for they have rejected the one who sent me. JOHN 15:21

DAY 11

A prayer about LIVING ONE DAY AT A TIME
When I remember I must follow Jesus daily

PRECIOUS SAVIOR,
When I gave my life to you, I know that was a once-forever experience. You forgave my sins—past, present, and future—gave me eternal life, and sent your Spirit to live in me. If I'm not careful, however, I can begin to rest in that and forget your challenge to *daily* follow you. As a finite human being, I am subject to the cycles of days, weeks, months, seasons, and years. And I'm growing and changing and working to meet the challenges that each one presents. I don't know why I think my spiritual life should be any different. My faith should be a day-by-day experience of turning away from sin, dying to self, and following you closely. You expect no instant saints, just faithful disciples who meet challenges and do as you say each and every day. Help me to see each new day as a fresh opportunity to take up my cross and follow you.

[Jesus] said to the crowd, "If any of you wants to be my follower, you must turn from your selfish ways, take up your cross daily, and follow me." LUKE 9:23

DAY 12

A prayer about NEEDS
When I worry about not having enough

DIVINE PROVIDER,

You give generously to me, so why do I worry about running out or not having enough for the future? Sometimes trusting you each day is difficult, Lord, and I can become tight fisted. Today I became aware of someone who needs financial help. I feel you urging me to open my checkbook, but according to my calculations, I'm running a bit short this month. I want to trust you, but letting go is a struggle. This has happened other times—a donor letter from a friend in Christian work, an appeal from a visiting missionary, an urgent request from an agency dealing with disaster victims, our church's general fund. And each time I have responded, you have blessed me with more than enough funds to cover my bills. Occasionally I daydream about having a windfall of money—then I certainly would be generous! But maybe not. And perhaps you're allowing me to have just enough so that I will learn to trust you more. So right now, before going to sleep, I am going to write that check I have been reluctant to write.

God will generously provide all you need. Then you will always have everything you need and plenty left over to share with others. 2 CORINTHIANS 9:8

DAY 13 *Prayerful Moment*

A prayer about SENSITIVITY TO SIN
When I know I've done wrong

HOLY SPIRIT,

One of your vital works is to convict of sin. When I do something wrong, I know because of your work in me. What do I do next? I need to repent, confess, and change my behavior. Thank you for your convicting work in me. I'm a sinner saved by grace, and I need your correction. Please give me the desire and strength to follow through.

If we confess our sins to him, he is faithful and just to forgive us our sins and to cleanse us from all wickedness.
1 JOHN 1:9

DAY 14 *Prayerful Moment*

A prayer about TRAGEDY
When calamity comes

MY GOD,

Daily I am reminded that the world is broken, marred by sin. As each catastrophe occurs worldwide, I grieve and pray for those affected. But I also assume that I am immune. Then, when tragedy strikes me, I am surprised. Forgive my self-centered attitude, Lord. Regardless of what happens, I know you are good all the time, and I praise your name.

People can never predict when hard times might come. Like fish in a net or birds in a trap, people are caught by sudden tragedy. ECCLESIASTES 9:12

DAY 15

A prayer about PERSECUTION
When I sense growing hostility to Christianity

DEAR GOD,
So far in my life with you, I have not suffered much for my faith. I can remember only a few times when someone made fun of me because of my stand for Christ. But I sense that our culture is becoming increasingly hostile to people of faith, especially Jesus followers. Tolerance is promoted as the highest value, but that usually means ABC—*a*nything *b*ut *C*hristian. Crosses and other Christian symbols are being removed from monuments, government buildings, businesses, and even cemeteries. Prayer is being purged from public gatherings. And I've heard stories of students being punished and people losing their jobs because they dared to share their faith. I can't help but wonder how I will respond, Lord, to persecution. Will I be ready? Will I react with grace, love, and joy? I want to be your person, God, everywhere. Help me to prepare now for whatever may come in the future. I want to be ready to suffer because of Jesus. I want to live for you and, if necessary, to die for you.

[Jesus said,] "Do you remember what I told you? 'A slave is not greater than the master.' Since they persecuted me, naturally they will persecute you. And if they had listened to me, they would listen to you." JOHN 15:20

DAY 16

A prayer about DESTINATION
When I live with purpose

GOD,

When I gave my life to Christ, it marked the *end* of what felt, at the time, like a long process. It was, after all, a journey toward you from my birth until then. I rejoiced in that moment, knowing that by faith I had been transformed, reborn, and adopted into your family. But in truth, that experience, my spiritual birth, was also the *beginning* of life together with you, as your child, and I began a lifetime walk in your direction. My life now has purpose and meaning because my goal is to honor you. At first they were baby steps, but each day I take more and longer steps with you, one at a time, focused on you and your will for me, always moving forward to reach your prize. Thank you, Lord, for saving me and diverting me from the wrong path of the power and penalty of sin, heading toward ultimate destruction. And thank you for leading every step toward my final destination, an eternity with you. I sleep, now, knowing my future is secure in you.

Don't you realize that in a race everyone runs, but only one person gets the prize? So run to win! All athletes are disciplined in their training. They do it to win a prize that will fade away, but we do it for an eternal prize. So I run with purpose in every step. I am not just shadowboxing. I discipline my body like an athlete, training it to do what it should. 1 CORINTHIANS 9:24-27

DAY 17

A prayer about BALANCE
When I need to order my life

DEAR GOD,
I notice that if I'm not careful, my life can begin to spin out of control, much like a lump of clay on a potter's wheel with too much clay on one side. I can spend so much time on the relational, social side of life that I neglect my emotional health or intellectual development. At other times, I can become so engrossed in learning that I neglect my relationships. And when I decide to shape up physically, those workouts can consume much of my time and interest. I can even pack my schedule with Christian activities and become unbalanced in that sector. When I read in the Gospel of Luke about Jesus' life, I see that he grew mentally, physically, spiritually, and socially—in all four areas. Like Jesus, I need balance, developing every facet of life, with him at the center of everything. Help me, Father, to be disciplined and to make wise choices, knowing when to say no and when to say yes. And help me see how you relate to *all* aspects of my life.

Jesus grew in wisdom and in stature and in favor with God and all the people. LUKE 2:52

DAY 18

A prayer about WEAKNESS
When I think about my shortcomings

HEAVENLY FATHER,
I am concerned about the image I project. I want people to think I am confident, gifted, and strong, that I have my act together. Certainly I have weaknesses and faults, but I hide them pretty well. Rather than letting many people see the real me, I try to reveal only my strengths and make good use of them. Yet the apostle Paul says that you were glorified through his weakness. Paul did not ask or want to be weak; in fact, he asked you three times to remove his "thorn." But you told him that your grace was all he needed and that your power "works best in weakness." After that, he was very open about his limitations and issues. To be honest, I'm not sure how to pray, Lord. I definitely desire your power to work through me, but does this require asking for problems, persecutions, and other difficulties? Yet if that's what it takes, then make me weak so you can work through me. I want to be your strong-weak person. Use me.

[God] said, "My grace is all you need. My power works best in weakness." So now I am glad to boast about my weaknesses, so that the power of Christ can work through me. That's why I take pleasure in my weaknesses, and in the insults, hardships, persecutions, and troubles that I suffer for Christ. For when I am weak, then I am strong.
2 CORINTHIANS 12:9-10

DAY 19

A prayer about CHILDREN

When I relate to the youngest generation

CHRIST JESUS,

I love babies, toddlers, and kids—watching them crawl, toddle, and walk; hearing their questions and detailed explanations. I am also enthralled when I observe their wonder as they discover their abilities and your creation. I welcome them into my world, as you told your disciples to do. But I am convicted by your words about causing "one of these little ones who trusts in [you] to fall into sin." Yes, they are sinners, but they are so innocent and vulnerable. And they look up to people like me, especially those with whom I spend lots of time teaching and coaching. These children are absorbing my values, repeating my words and expressions, and copying my actions. I remember, as a child, admiring the older kid in the neighborhood, my Sunday school teacher, and special aunts and uncles. I know that I have the holy responsibility of living out what it means to follow you, of being a Jesus role model. So I pray that when children watch me, may they see someone who loves, serves, gives, and puts you first.

Jesus called a little child to him and put the child among them. Then he said, . . . "Anyone who welcomes a little child like this on my behalf is welcoming me. But if you cause one of these little ones who trusts in me to fall into sin, it would be better for you to have a large millstone tied around your neck and be drowned in the depths of the sea."

MATTHEW 18:2-3, 5-6

DAY 20 *Prayerful Moment*

A prayer about LEGACY
When I ponder what I will leave behind

JESUS,
Please show me how to build into the next generation. I want to leave a legacy of faith. This begins at my relationship with you; show me how I should live so others will see you in me. Give me opportunities to mentor younger believers. This task is for all who name you, including me.

You must commit yourselves wholeheartedly to these commands that I am giving you today. Repeat them again and again to your children.
DEUTERONOMY 6:6-7

DAY 21 *Prayerful Moment*

A prayer about A CLEAN HEART
When I recognize my guilt before God

GRACIOUS HEAVENLY FATHER,
Confronted with his terrible sins, David was devastated. Broken and contrite, he confessed and asked you to remove the "stain" of his guilt. Sin stains me deeply, too, Lord. I know that Jesus died for me and that my sins are forgiven, but I want a clean heart. Scrubbed, rinsed, purified, I want to follow you wholeheartedly. Forgive me, Father, for wanting anything but your perfect will.

Don't keep looking at my sins. Remove the stain of my guilt. Create in me a clean heart, O God. Renew a loyal spirit within me. PSALM 51:9-10

A prayer about ASSURANCE
When I am questioning my faith

MY LORD AND MY GOD,
I have often sung this verse of one of Fanny Crosby's classic hymns: "Blessed assurance, Jesus is mine! O what a foretaste of glory divine! Heir of salvation, purchase of God, born of His Spirit, washed in His blood." I sincerely mean every word, but at times my assurance doesn't seem very "blessed" when I'm questioning my faith. An emotionally draining conflict can bring doubts. Tragic events can get me wondering about your love. Or I can simply become complacent and coast in the Christian life. That's when I need to return to the truth of my relationship with you, facts found in that favorite verse: I'm an heir; I have been bought; I am a new person, born again; because of the Cross I am forgiven, clean! That is "my story," "my song." O God, continually remind me that my faith is based on the finished work of Christ, and that whenever I feel unnerved by swirling events or doubts that assault my mind, I can remember the truth. And I can praise my Savior, "all the day long!"

You must continue to believe this truth and stand firmly in it. Don't drift away from the assurance you received when you heard the Good News. COLOSSIANS 1:23

DAY 23

A prayer about GOD'S SUPPORT
When I discover a profound Bible promise

HEAVENLY FATHER,

As I read the eighth chapter of Romans, a small phrase got my attention. I have read this passage many times, but at this reading, I stopped to consider the implications. Just four words, but loaded with promise—I read, "God is for us." And I thought, *You are for me*. What a positive note of encouragement. You are not neutral or "against" or angry—you are interested, involved, and want success, the very best. And then it gets personal: you are for *me*. Wow! The eternal, all powerful, all knowing, sovereign God is on my side, working with me, on my behalf, encouraging me to succeed. It is as though you are cheering me on throughout life's race as my biggest fan. Or as someone has said, my picture is on your refrigerator. What can I say, Lord? I know I don't deserve your love, your favor. But in your grace you give it. Paul asks a rhetorical question: "What shall we say about such wonderful things as these?" Then he answers it: "If God is for us, who can ever be against us?" No one. Hallelujah!

What shall we say about such wonderful things as these? If God is for us, who can ever be against us? ROMANS 8:31

DAY 24

A prayer about REST
When I am tired

LORD,

Yesterday was fairly normal, and today began all right. In fact, I was cheerful and optimistic as I arose and prepared. But now I'm exhausted—worn out and worn down by the cares and concerns of the last twelve hours. Everyone seemed to want a piece of me, as I dealt with in-person conversations, phone calls, meetings, and messages. Frantically I worked to meet demands, filling every minute. I have accomplished much, but I have left much undone. And I feel spent and just want to escape this exhausting routine. I fear that this weariness of body and soul is encroaching on other areas of my life: my relationships with people, my perspective, and most important, my relationship with you. Father, you have promised to be my Divine Shepherd, to feed me, lead me, and restore me. I pray for that right now. I need the rest you promise; I need you. Please help me fall back in total trust. Catch me and enfold me with your love. Give my soul peace tonight. Then help me awaken and arise, strengthened to live fully for you.

The LORD is my shepherd; I have all that I need. He lets me rest in green meadows; he leads me beside peaceful streams. He renews my strength. PSALM 23:1-3

A prayer about TITHING
When I give back to God

GOD ABOVE,
All I have comes from you. How then could I ever hold back from you anything meant to be used in your service? I admit that I am tempted, Lord, to do just that, especially when the offering plate is passed and my funds are low. Through the prophet Malachi you made very clear that the people were cheating you. They needed to present their tithes (10 percent) to the Temple for your work, but they were resisting. Do I ever cheat you, God? Forgive me for being cheap with you. I should give joyfully and gratefully, not out of obligation or guilt. I also need to change my monthly procedures and write the checks to the church and other ministries *first*, instead of waiting to see what is left over. And I should give generously from all my resources, not just financial. Teach me, Lord. Use tithing to stretch my faith.

[The Lord said,] "Should people cheat God? Yet you have cheated me! But you ask, 'What do you mean? When did we ever cheat you?' You have cheated me of the tithes and offerings due to me. . . . Bring all the tithes into the storehouse so there will be enough food in my Temple. If you do," says the LORD of Heaven's Armies, "I will open the windows of heaven for you. I will pour out a blessing so great you won't have enough room to take it in! Try it! Put me to the test!"
MALACHI 3:8, 10

DAY 26

A prayer about PROBLEM SOLVING

When I need to correct or resolve an issue

HEAVENLY FATHER,

I have always seen myself as a problem solver, a fixer. When I see something that needs fixing, I check out the situation, analyze it, decide what needs to happen, and get it done. I confess that I often attempt this on my own, trying plans A to Z until I'm out of options. Then I turn in desperation to you and ask for your help. Please forgive me for that approach. Instead of last, you should be my *first* resort, mainly because I want to live your way and because you are the ultimate Problem Solver. Nothing is beyond your wisdom and power. You can lead me to the right solution, whether that is plan A, B, or whatever. You know I am facing a difficult problem. More than a sticky situation, to me it looks insurmountable, impossible. But with you all things are possible. So I ask for wisdom to know what to do. What approach should I take? Whose help should I enlist? Please lead me and strengthen me for the task.

Jesus looked at them intently and said, "Humanly speaking, it is impossible. But not with God. Everything is possible with God." MARK 10:27

DAY 27 *Prayerful Moment*

A prayer about DECISIONS
When I have critical choices to make

DEAR LORD,

I am facing turning points, some big choices, and the path isn't clear. I need wisdom to know which way to go. In all my decisions, big and small, I want to obey your Word, to honor you. Open my mind to understand what you want me to do. Then give me the will to do it, to obey you in all areas of my life.

The LORD grants wisdom! From his mouth come knowledge and understanding. . . . For wisdom will enter your heart, and knowledge will fill you with joy. Wise choices will watch over you. PROVERBS 2:6, 10-11

DAY 28 *Prayerful Moment*

A prayer about DISCIPLINE
When I need the Father's correction

ALMIGHTY GOD,

You love me with a perfect love, so why do I resist your guidance and fear your loving discipline? I usually do not flagrantly disobey you, but I am prone to lukewarm indifference. Teach me, dear Father, and lead me, even if the way is rough. I know you want only what is best for me, and I humbly submit to your holy will. Please keep me on your path of righteousness.

Just as a parent disciplines a child, the LORD your God disciplines you for your own good. DEUTERONOMY 8:5

DAY 29

A prayer about JOY
When I want to truly enjoy life

MARVELOUS LORD,
I love to laugh and enjoy a good joke. My favorite shows, movies, and plays are comedies. And like everyone else, I want a happy life. I know firsthand, however, that the days, months, and years are not all filled with laughter and good feelings. Sin, sickness, and disasters run rampant in this fallen world, and all people, me included, are susceptible. Some days are tougher than others, and today was one of those days. Although I enjoy the laughs, I want to go deeper, Lord—I want *joy*. I want joy in living, in relationships, in my future hopes and dreams, and most of all, in my salvation. Joy comes from the deep assurance that you are sovereign, so despite my present circumstances, I know you are here and in control. Joy comes from remembering that you love me, are not angry with me, and have a glorious future planned for me. Joy comes from the profound knowledge that I am forgiven, saved, and bound for heaven. Joy comes from knowing and serving Jesus. Praise you, Lord!

Praise the LORD! For he has heard my cry for mercy. The LORD is my strength and shield. I trust him with all my heart. He helps me, and my heart is filled with joy. I burst out in songs of thanksgiving. PSALM 28:6-7

DAY 30

A prayer about EVERYDAY MIRACLES
When I see God working around me

JESUS,

I have fond memories of the great stories of the Bible where you intervened on behalf of your people, often using everyday people such as Noah, Moses, Joshua, Gideon, David, Shadrach, Meshach, and Abednego. Bible history is replete with miracles: victories, judgment, divine messages, provision, protection, prophecies, paths through swirling waters, fire from heaven, and more. And you calmed the storm; healed the sick, blind, and lame; walked on water; multiplied a child's lunch to feed thousands; raised the dead; and exorcized demons, restoring broken lives and bringing hope to the multitudes. After your resurrection and ascent to heaven, you continued to empower the disciples. But because that happened so long ago, I tend to think that the age of miracles must have passed. If I keep my eyes and ears open, however, I'll sense your miraculous work all around me: love, conception, birth, health, rescue, answered prayer, salvation—lives forever changed by grace through faith. Amazingly, you are working in me, and you allow me to participate in this work. Thank you, Savior.

[Jesus said,] "I tell you the truth, anyone who believes in me will do the same works I have done, and even greater works, because I am going to be with the Father."

JOHN 14:12

DAY 31

A prayer about OBSTACLES

When obstructions and barriers block my way

GRACIOUS HEAVENLY FATHER,

You know I want to do your will. But lately I have encountered more than the usual amount of hindrances. These can be small interruptions in my schedule, people needing something done "immediately," forcing me to rearrange my day. These can also be irritants such as weather, car trouble, computer glitches, and traffic jams. Those problems seem to have increased the last few days. And on a much larger scale I have new obstacles that obstruct my view of you and barriers that block my way. These are of an interpersonal nature mostly—conflicts and complaints (many manufactured) that require my attention and drain my energy and emotion. There is drama on all sides. If this is spiritual warfare, bind Satan, I pray, so that he does not hinder my work for you. Please remove these obstacles, Lord, unless you have placed them to stop or redirect me. In that case, I ask for discernment and for strength. And please keep me from discouragement, remembering your promises and sensing your presence as I do your work for your glory.

I can do everything through Christ, who gives me strength.
PHILIPPIANS 4:13

A prayer about LIGHT
When I am in the dark

GRACIOUS GOD,
Today I was reminded that this world is a dark place. With reports of drug abuse, gangs, random killings, promiscuity, and wholesale rejection of your moral law, I can almost feel evil closing in, like a huge, heavy cloud blocking the sun. The scene is ominous, menacing, evoking a sense of dread and fear. Isaiah wrote of people walking in darkness—confused and bound for disaster—but he said the light would come. And Jesus is that light, the Light of the world. Light illuminates, spotlights, and guides. Most important, light dispels the dark. The absence of light can lead to doubt, injury, and despair. That's where Satan wants me to live, so that he can set the parameters for my life. But Jesus breaks through and offers hope and the way to life. So with Jesus, the Light, I have a choice: I can remain in the darkness, or I can follow him and walk in the light, as he leads the way to life. I choose the Light. Please help me, Lord, to stay focused on him.

Jesus spoke to the people . . . and said, "I am the light of the world. If you follow me, you won't have to walk in darkness, because you will have the light that leads to life."
JOHN 8:12

DAY 33

A prayer about FORTITUDE
When I need staying power

O LORD,

Another Christian leader just confessed to a moral failing. This person had been at the heights and then came crashing down. I can't imagine the damage inflicted by this person—to family, friends, and students—because of the affair. This leader was a role model, a hero, to so many. The situation reminds me of Demas, mentioned in 2 Timothy. He started strong, a fellow minister with Luke and Paul, but then was drawn away by the "things of this life." My first response was to be indignant and judgmental, but then I thought, *That could be me. I'm not invulnerable or invincible.* I don't want to be a moral and spiritual casualty, Lord. I know I am weak, and at times the temptations hit full force. So I pray, Father, for strength to resist and for power, *staying* power—fortitude. People look up to me and are counting on me, so I need to be strong for them. It's my responsibility as a spiritual leader. Most important, I need to be strong for you. I want to be like the apostle Paul, not like Demas.

Demas has deserted me [Paul] because he loves the things of this life and has gone to Thessalonica. 2 TIMOTHY 4:10

DAY 34 *Prayerful Moment*

A prayer about PRIDE
When I begin to think too highly of myself

LORD JESUS,
Today I seemed to inject myself into every conversation, wanting to make sure that I got the credit I felt I deserved. How foolish! Forgive me. I want to be your humble servant, not one who is into self-promotion. Keeping my eyes focused on your nature and selfless sacrifice, Lord, gives me a true picture of myself and my place in your plan. I want to do your work, with your strength, to the best of my ability—for *your* glory, not mine.

Pride leads to disgrace, but with humility comes wisdom.
PROVERBS 11:2

DAY 35 *Prayerful Moment*

A prayer about RISK
When I would rather play it safe

HEAVENLY FATHER,
I am impressed with the people of faith in the Bible who took great risks to obey you and to spread the Good News about Jesus. I confess that I often play it safe. Rather than risk conflict or ridicule, I deny you by my silence. I pray for courage, Lord, to stand for you.

All these people earned a good reputation because of their faith, yet none of them received all that God had promised.
HEBREWS 11:39

DAY 36

A prayer about MERCY TOWARD OTHERS
When I desire increased empathy for others' needs

ALMIGHTY GOD,
I admit it—I am angry right now for the way I have been treated. I was wronged, grievously, and thoughts of retaliation and revenge fill my mind. I know I'm supposed to leave that to you, let go, forgive, and move on. But this person owes me a huge debt, and I want payment. That's how I feel. I also find myself becoming calloused to others' needs, even prayer requests from friends and others on the church prayer chain. What's wrong with me that I cannot feel with them, pray for them, and help them? I am so disappointed in myself, especially knowing that I am to be like you and that you have shown great mercy to me for so long and in so many ways. Please give me a heart filled with mercy, making me slow to get angry and quick to forgive, just as you have forgiven me. And give me a sensitive and sincere spirit, quick to respond to others in their times of need, just as you continuously show your love for me.

You must show mercy to those whose faith is wavering. Rescue others by snatching them from the flames of judgment. Show mercy to still others, but do so with great caution, hating the sins that contaminate their lives. JUDE 1:22-23

DAY 37

A prayer about DELAY

When I am tempted to slow down my obedience

HOLY SPIRIT,

I usually live by the motto "Do it now" because I like to prioritize tasks and check them off my list. I'm a doer more than a talker. I also know that things undone tend to pile up until they are buried, and I never get to them. So my desk is clean. For some reason, however, I find myself delaying in my obedience to you. That is, I know what you want me to do, but I don't "do it now." Instead, I put it off and leave it for later. Yet at the same time, I seem to be quick to respond the wrong way—quick to speak in anger. I have it backward. Why do I find doing what is wrong so easy and doing what is right so difficult? And then, when I think about what I haven't gotten around to do, I make excuses, usually about being busy. How ironic! Please forgive me, I pray. And do your work in me, Spirit, giving me the will and strength to obey you immediately, without delay.

I will hurry, without delay, to obey your commands.

PSALM 119:60

DAY 38

A prayer about my CRITICAL SPIRIT
When I look at life through a negative lens

HEAVENLY FATHER,
Lately being happy or even content has been difficult for me. I know the world is not perfect—I certainly am far from perfection—but I seem to expect it in others. Being a perfectionist is not good in a sinful, imperfect world. Individuals' faults seem to jump out at me—I see them clearly. And I don't like what I hear from elected officials to weather forecasters or the treatment I receive from store clerks and restaurant staff. Even worse, I often open my mouth and voice my observations and thoughts to anyone who will listen. This attitude has spilled over into my church life, and these days I seem to criticize everyone and everything: the teaching is boring, the worship songs are too old or too new, the preaching isn't deep, the child nearby is too noisy . . . I don't like the kind of person I'm becoming, Father. Please remove my critical spirit. Give me your perspective, focusing on my blessings and the good in others. And help me celebrate all your gifts.

Let us aim for harmony in the church and try to build each other up. ROMANS 14:19

DAY 39

A prayer about ILLUMINATION
When I read and teach God's Word

SPIRIT OF GOD,
I believe that the Bible is revealed by God, so it is inspired. All Scripture is inerrant, totally accurate in all that it reports and teaches. That's why I read the Bible regularly in daily devotions and small group studies and listen to the Word preached and taught in church. Because the Bible is more than merely a very large book, I need to work at understanding the meaning of its spiritual truths, discerning the timeless principles, and seeing how they apply to me. I can't do this on my own; I need you, Holy Spirit. Without you, I would only be reading words on a page. Open my spiritual eyes, I pray, to help me see the wonderful truths in your Word. Lead me to those passages that I need for my correction and for guidance. And Lord, give me the words to say when I teach others from the Bible. I don't want to be known as a clever person or a good speaker, but as one who hears from you and then opens the Word.

Be good to your servant, that I may live and obey your word. Open my eyes to see the wonderful truths in your instructions. PSALM 119:17-18

A prayer about GLORIFYING GOD
When I think about life's mundane tasks

HEAVENLY FATHER,
Often I act as though you are interested only in my spiritual activities such as praying, reading my Bible, tithing, worshiping, teaching Sunday school, and sharing my faith. But I also know you want to be involved in the big issues in my life: my choices and actions at home, with friends, on the job, in church, around the neighborhood, and in the community. Certainly I need to consider your will in those places and honor you in how I think, speak, and act. But life consists mostly of the small and mundane, the routines of daily living: preparing for the day, eating, driving, cleaning the house, answering e-mails, talking on the phone, exercising, cutting the grass, shoveling snow, planting flowers, shopping. I also know that you want me to do it all for your glory. Please help me to remember that personal exhortation, Lord. You are interested and involved in every detail of my life, and I want to glorify you in all things big, small, and in between—with every breath and in every situation.

Whether you eat or drink, or whatever you do, do it all for the glory of God. 1 CORINTHIANS 10:31

DAY 41 *Prayerful Moment*

A prayer about HELP
When I am weak

ALMIGHTY GOD,
As a small child I remember singing "Jesus Loves Me" and the familiar refrain, "They are weak, but he is strong." For a while, I resonated with that verse because "little ones" are, in fact, quite weak. But now I know that *all* of us—regardless of age, maturity, or status—are weak. I am nothing without you and can do nothing at all on my own. But you are *strong*, and you promise to empower those who rely on you. I need you. Help!

God arms me with strength, and he makes my way perfect.
PSALM 18:32

DAY 42 *Prayerful Moment*

A prayer about INSECURITY
When I am feeling unsettled, unsure

SOVEREIGN LORD,
I know in my mind that you are in control, that nothing catches you by surprise. Everything that happens is within your permissive will. But recent events have unnerved me: terrorism, the broken economy, school shootings, and more. I want to face each day knowing you are watching over me. Please give me a renewed sense of your presence.

Those who trust in the LORD are as secure as Mount Zion; they will not be defeated but will endure forever.
PSALM 125:1

A prayer about LOVE FOR ENEMIES

When I interact with those who stand against me

JESUS,

Today I was reflecting on your statement about loving enemies. I don't have any "sworn enemies," people who are out to get me, such as an opposing army with weapons. And I've never encountered severe persecution similar to what your disciples encountered. I do, however, have opponents, adversaries, and rivals—people who continually stand against me, seeming to oppose everything I say and do. Some criticize me publicly and gossip behind my back. I have heard about people who have been terribly wronged, even harmed physically, who then forgave those who hurt them. And I've read about persecuted Christians who have forgiven their captors and torturers. I don't know how they do it, Lord, because I seem to respond with only dislike and hatred for my enemies. I know that's not your way. And I remember your cry from the cross, asking your Father to forgive those who were crucifying you. So right now I pray for these personal aggravating enemies: I ask that you bless them. And please help me respond to their taunts and insults with love.

You have heard the law that says, "Love your neighbor" and hate your enemy. But I say, love your enemies! Pray for those who persecute you! MATTHEW 5:43-44

DAY 44

A prayer about HEAVEN
When I think about the future

FATHER,

All my life I've heard about heaven—in sermons, at funerals, and more. I have read about pearly gates and streets of gold and St. Peter meeting everyone. I've seen depictions of people in heaven sporting wings and sitting on clouds. Sometimes determining fact from fiction can be difficult. Whatever the specifics, I know heaven is real, and I will live there forever, after I die, because Jesus died for me and I have given my life to him. It will also be beyond anything I can imagine, certainly not boring. Like most people, I fear death because what happens, exactly, is a mystery. I am especially afraid that a loved one will die. So I rest on your promise, Lord, that heaven is real and that one day I will be reunited with family and friends who know you and with all who have trusted Christ through the centuries. Help me hold on to that hope, that assurance. And Lord, I pray for those who don't know you. Help me be a strong witness of the reality of eternal life.

All praise to God, the Father of our Lord Jesus Christ. It is by his great mercy that we have been born again, because God raised Jesus Christ from the dead. Now we live with great expectation, and we have a priceless inheritance—an inheritance that is kept in heaven for you, pure and undefiled, beyond the reach of change and decay. And through your faith, God is protecting you by his power until you receive this salvation. 1 PETER 1:3-5

DAY 45

A prayer about MEETING MY NEEDS
When I should be more others centered

DEAR JESUS,

I'm a needy person. Like anyone else, I want people to like me and to say good things about me. But sometimes my needs get in the way, and I begin to concentrate almost exclusively on myself. You were never like that; instead, you humbled yourself and even washed the disciples' feet. Then you told them to follow your example. You also taught that we shouldn't push for the best seats in the house and that the first will be last. Yet I can lapse into a me-first attitude. Instead, I need to remember your words and actions and follow your example. I can see the problem in others, and even think, *Whose needs are being met here?* But I can be blind to my own behavior in this regard—until I look back and see how I acted. So please sensitize me to this tendency, Jesus, and help me do what is right and others centered. And make this a normal and sincere part of my life, not a rule to follow. I need to grow in this area.

Don't be selfish; don't try to impress others. Be humble, thinking of others as better than yourselves. Don't look out only for your own interests, but take an interest in others, too. PHILIPPIANS 2:3-4

DAY 46

A prayer about TEACHING
When I need to learn

DEAR GOD,

I do not see myself as harsh, dogmatic, or closed minded, but I admit that I can have strong opinions about certain issues. At times, this can make being open to another view or to new information difficult. Recently I have noticed that this tendency has crept into my responsiveness to teaching, especially when listening to Bible teachers. Instead of having an open mind and heart, I listen critically, looking for flaws in the presentation. Or I can close off from the teaching by negating the teacher, thinking, *What does this person know anyway?* Forgive me, Lord. Certainly I need to think and to check the teaching with Scripture, but I should be receptive to helpful input, solid content, and life-challenging applications from other students of your Word. I *do not* know it all and shouldn't act as though I do. I want to continue to learn and grow in my faith. Please lead me to those who can help in this process. And if I have opportunities to teach, help me do it with integrity and humility.

Intelligent people are always ready to learn. Their ears are open for knowledge. PROVERBS 18:15

DAY 47

A prayer about WORDS THAT HURT
When my speech causes pain

DEAR GOD,

I'm a words person. I use them to persuade, sell, bargain, and challenge. I think I write fairly well and have a decent vocabulary. Unfortunately, today I used this gift in a way you did not intend. I used words to cut someone down to size. It was an insulting e-mail quickly composed and sent. Soon after, I regretted my action, but the damage had been done. Now I have to repair that relationship—please help me. This incident reminded me of similar occasions of ripping others with my words. In those moments, my mind quickly releases hateful expressions that become weapons. On other occasions I meant no harm, but thoughtless comments caused pain. Sometimes I wonder about the source of those words and how I can be so insensitive and even cruel. Certainly they flow from my sinful nature, so I need your restraining power, Lord. Please show me a better way to express my displeasure without attacking the person. Even when I know I am right or have been wronged, may my words be filled with grace.

I [David] said to myself, "I will watch what I do and not sin in what I say. I will hold my tongue when the ungodly are around me." But as I stood there in silence—not even speaking of good things—the turmoil within me grew worse. The more I thought about it, the hotter I got, igniting a fire of words. PSALM 39:1-3

DAY 48 *Prayerful Moment*

A prayer about KINDNESS
When I want to pass on the goodness of others

FATHER,
Several times today people were extremely helpful. Their voluntary attitude and acts of kindness made me think of how I treat people at times. I can easily walk by someone in need or only half listen to a friend's plight. And I can hold a grudge after a minor slight. I want to be like Christ—kind, tenderhearted, and quick to forgive.

Be kind to each other, tenderhearted, forgiving one another, just as God through Christ has forgiven you.
EPHESIANS 4:32

DAY 49 *Prayerful Moment*

A prayer about VULNERABILITY
When I feel helpless

LOVING FATHER,
I feel so vulnerable right now, totally open, exposed, and helpless. With all that I have been going through, my emotions are raw. Even more than comfort, Lord, right now I need your peace and protection. Please guard me from myself—I'm afraid of what I might do or say—and from others who might try to take advantage of me. I am trusting fully in you because you are all I have.

LORD, who can compare with you? Who else rescues the helpless from the strong? Who else protects the helpless and poor from those who rob them? PSALM 35:10

A prayer about KNOWING CHRIST
When I want to deepen my faith in Christ

DEAR JESUS,
I earnestly proclaim with Paul that I want to "know Christ" and the "mighty power that raised him from the dead." I realize that Paul also added suffering and death to the equation. He already knew you in terms of his Christianity—as with all believers, he had a personal relationship with you by grace through faith. He also knew the truth about your resurrection from the dead and based his life on it. But here he goes deeper and further, expressing his desire to be totally identified with you. Again, I can easily mouth those words, but am I willing to suffer and die because I am a follower of yours? Nothing I experience in this life will come close to what you endured for me, becoming sin, judged guilty, and crucified in my place. But I do want to be counted worthy to suffer for you. I can get frustrated with small inconveniences and injuries, so please give me courage and strength to endure any physical and emotional suffering that may come. I want to *know* you, Lord.

I become righteous through faith in Christ. For God's way of making us right with himself depends on faith. I want to know Christ and experience the mighty power that raised him from the dead. I want to suffer with him, sharing in his death, so that one way or another I will experience the resurrection from the dead! PHILIPPIANS 3:9-11

A prayer about SPIRITUAL WARFARE
When I understand the real battle

DEAR GOD,

I have heard warnings about being in a spiritual war, and now I have experienced it. I was hit from all sides: unexpected setbacks, whispered doubts, twisted facts, false accusations, strong temptations, and roadblocks to doing your will. I couldn't see the enemy, but the evil forces were real and intense. Although the enemy has mighty powers, he is no match for you, almighty God. I cannot win this battle on my own; I need you to strengthen and equip me. You have told me to wear your armor—truth, righteousness, peace, faith, and salvation—to defend against Satan's attacks. But you also want me to take the offensive, wielding your Word as a sword. So Lord, I resolve to stand firm in your mighty power, holding to the truth, secure in my relationship with you, trusting you fully, and living to glorify you. I will attack evil with your inspired promises and declarations. Together we will prevail.

Be strong in the Lord and in his mighty power. Put on all of God's armor so that you will be able to stand firm against all strategies of the devil. For we are not fighting against flesh-and-blood enemies, but against evil rulers and authorities of the unseen world, against mighty powers in this dark world, and against evil spirits in the heavenly places. Therefore, put on every piece of God's armor so you will be able to resist the enemy in the time of evil. Then after the battle you will still be standing firm. EPHESIANS 6:10-13

DAY 52

A prayer about KEEPING PROMISES
When I pledge to do something

MY FATHER IN HEAVEN,

You are a promise-making and promise-keeping God. I can always depend on you completely. Thank you for keeping your promises to me. I know you want me to be careful with my words and then stand behind them with actions, but I often fail to do so. Instead, I make excuses or claim that I have changed my mind. I have even told people, earnestly and sincerely, that I will pray for them, only to forget their prayer requests. I openly profess that I will be your devoted follower, but then I don't keep my word. And that sullies your name. Much worse, I have broken promises I made to you. I remember pledging to never again do a certain sin—but I did. I promised to tithe, to read your Word regularly, to serve others, and to boldly share the Good News, but those statements were soon abandoned. Please do what is necessary to mold me into a person of my word, of truth and integrity.

When you make a promise to God, don't delay in following through, for God takes no pleasure in fools. Keep all the promises you make to him. It is better to say nothing than to make a promise and not keep it. Don't let your mouth make you sin. And don't defend yourself by telling the Temple messenger that the promise you made was a mistake. That would make God angry, and he might wipe out everything you have achieved. Talk is cheap, like daydreams and other useless activities. ECCLESIASTES 5:4-7

DAY 53

A prayer about HAPPINESS

When I want to enjoy life

MY SAVIOR,

According to the Declaration of Independence, the pursuit of happiness is supposed to be an "unalienable right"—belonging to everyone, naturally and legally. I certainly see people working hard to obtain this elusive experience, perhaps as their own way to declare their independence. I've also heard parents say about their children, "I just want them to be happy." That sounds good, and I want happiness too; but I don't see many good options in the world for the kind that I desire. Most people's happiness doesn't last very long, probably because it is based on short-lived pleasures and experiences such as partying hard, having a great vacation, or owning the latest electronic toy. None of those are necessarily bad, but they are poor substitutes for the real thing. According to your Word and my experience, true happiness is found only in doing your will—living close to you and living your way. Keep me from following trivial pursuits. Totally dependent on you, I want the happiness that only you can bring.

Make me walk along the path of your commands, for that is where my happiness is found. PSALM 119:35

DAY 54

A prayer about HOLINESS

When I think about being set apart to God

HOLY GOD,

Time and again I read in Scripture that you want your people to be sanctified, holy. I know this means you want us to be set apart from the rest of the world, completely devoted to you. We should be different from the rest of society by our behavior, certainly. This involves not doing particular things and doing others such as going to church, helping people, reading the Bible, and so forth. But it also means having a different outlook on life, with values, priorities, and motives that honor you. I'm afraid that I fall short, and at times, very little in my life distinguishes me as being your child, a part of your holy people. I know I'm not perfect and never will be until I see you face-to-face. But you want me to "be holy in everything [I] do." I am a sinner, but I have been forgiven and declared not guilty. And now the Holy Spirit resides in me, helping me become more and more like Christ. I want to be holy and wholly yours.

You must be holy in everything you do, just as God who chose you is holy. For the Scriptures say, "You must be holy because I am holy." 1 PETER 1:15-16

DAY 55 *Prayerful Moment*

A prayer about HEART TROUBLES
When I know the love of my life

JESUS,

I love you because you first loved me and gave your life to save me from sin. Yet at times, I am enticed by other potential heart suitors. But the offers of these false gods are lies. Forgive me for even looking. My heart belongs to you alone. Proverbs points out that my top priority should be to guard my heart, so as not to weaken my loyalty and commitment. Help me, Savior, to keep close to you.

Guard your heart above all else, for it determines the course of your life. PROVERBS 4:23

DAY 56 *Prayerful Moment*

A prayer about TURMOIL
When chaos reigns

MY SOVEREIGN GOD,

Lately I have felt like the disciples on the Sea of Galilee, tossed about by the wind and the raging sea. Everything is in turmoil and I feel as though I am about to fall under the waves. Just as Jesus was with the disciples in their boat, I know you are with me. Please, God, still my anxious heart and bring calm to the chaos.

The disciples went and woke him up, shouting, "Master, Master, we're going to drown!" When Jesus woke up, he rebuked the wind and the raging waves. Suddenly the storm stopped and all was calm. LUKE 8:24

DAY 57

A prayer about REGRETS
When I begin to dwell on my past

HOLY SPIRIT,

Occasionally I think about past events and decisions and wonder "What if . . . " or "If only . . . ," which fills my mind with questions and regrets. That can be good if I learn from my mistakes, but it can be debilitating if I dwell on the past. That would be "worldly sorrow," which would lead me away from you. I shouldn't allow Satan to accuse me and remind me of my sins. You have forgiven me, Lord, and I must remember that truth, praise you for your mercy and grace, and move on. Another of Satan's tactics is to create a longing for the life I left behind when I began to follow you, much like what the children of Israel did on their way to the Promised Land, forgetting the chains in Egypt and longing for the "pleasures." How foolish, unproductive, and insulting to you. Please give me strength and determination to resist that urge and to focus on you, remembering that you have redeemed and rescued me and are leading me home.

The kind of sorrow God wants us to experience leads us away from sin and results in salvation. There's no regret for that kind of sorrow. But worldly sorrow, which lacks repentance, results in spiritual death. 2 CORINTHIANS 7:10

DAY 58

A prayer about EGO

When I crave the spotlight and credit

GOD,

I admit that I have a big ego. I can become almost obsessed with *my* personal situations and needs. I also can spend way too much time worrying about others' perceptions of me, wanting them to appreciate what I've done and making sure that I get credit for my accomplishments. A healthy self-concept is important to have, but a prideful approach and arrogance are wrong. I know that I am special to you, but I need to keep this ego in check . . . and I need your help. I also admit that at times I push others down to elevate myself or clamor to be in the spotlight, and that's sinful. Forgive me, Lord. I want to have an accurate, God's-eye view of myself, willingly sharing the spotlight and letting others take credit, even for my work. Please keep me from arrogance and the obsession with *my* wants and needs. Give me a humble spirit, willing to submit to you first and then to others. Let my life shine on you.

Human pride will be brought down, and human arrogance will be humbled. Only the LORD will be exalted on that day of judgment. ISAIAH 2:11

DAY 59

A prayer about TEMPTATION
When I feel the urge to do wrong

LOVING GOD,
Please keep me from overconfidence in my ability to withstand temptation. I need *always* to depend on you. Every day I am presented with opportunities to make wrong choices. These may include compromising my integrity, not telling the truth, stealing, gossiping, seeking revenge, meeting my needs through another person, elevating myself, or becoming involved in sexual immorality. I am a fallible, sinful human being, vulnerable to these pressures. I know the temptations do not come from you but from Satan and my sinful nature. At times, they are strong and can seem almost irresistible. But you have promised to not allow me to be tempted more than I can stand. I claim that promise, Lord, knowing you are faithful and true. You also said that with each temptation you will provide an escape route, an obvious way to reject or avoid it. So when I am tempted, help me to be grateful for the opportunity. Thank you, God, for trusting me this much! Then please show me the way out and give me the courage and power to take it.

If you think you are standing strong, be careful not to fall. The temptations in your life are no different from what others experience. And God is faithful. He will not allow the temptation to be more than you can stand. When you are tempted, he will show you a way out so that you can endure. 1 CORINTHIANS 10:12-13

DAY 60

A prayer about EMOTIONS
When my feelings swing wildly

HOLY SPIRIT,
I remember watching friends get all excited over a small gift or embittered over a perceived slight. I thought how foolish they were to allow circumstances and feelings to make or break their day. But lately I have been doing the same thing. Emotions are tricky because they can be intense and can swing to extremes. I don't think I'm overly emotional, and I don't make major decisions based on my feelings. But I have been on an emotional roller coaster ride—up and then suddenly down and with many twists and turns between. Bad news gets me upset; then I'm over the edge in the other direction when something good happens. I seem to be at the mercy of circumstances and my feelings. Holy Spirit, please do your work in me, illuminating your inspired Word, showing me truth, and putting me on an even keel. I don't want to stuff or deny my emotions, Lord, but I need to get them under control—under *your* control. Please work in my mind and heart, transforming me into a disciple who is feeling and caring, but also thoughtful and steady.

Our actions will show that we belong to the truth, so we will be confident when we stand before God. Even if we feel guilty, God is greater than our feelings, and he knows everything. 1 JOHN 3:19-20

DAY 61

A prayer about LOOSENING MY GRIP
When I hold on to what doesn't matter

GOD,
Please help me loosen my grip on things that don't matter and tighten my grip on those that do. Reflecting back on the day and the previous days and weeks, I'm afraid that often I have it all backward, majoring in the minors instead. From time to time, for example, in various relationships I become annoyed or insulted over an unintended slight. At times my schedule, my to-do list, seems more important than caring for others. Even at church, I find my mind wandering away from worship and toward insignificant issues and concerns. Tightening my grip on what matters most means making sure that nothing comes between you and me, that I keep our relationship at the top of my priorities. It also means thinking about whether my life honors you. By watching me, people should be able to see Jesus or, at least, someone trying to be like him. And I should always value people over any possession. By your Spirit, give me the courage to hold things loosely and the strength to hold firmly to you.

You must love the LORD your God with all your heart, all your soul, and all your strength. DEUTERONOMY 6:5

DAY 62 *Prayerful Moment*

A prayer about MATURITY
When I analyze my growth in faith

HOLY SPIRIT,
I want to grow up in the faith. The easy and convenient way is to settle for a diet of milk alone. But I have grown and changed, and I want to mature in my relationship with you. This means getting spiritual nourishment through solid preaching, teaching, and Bible study. It also means stretching my faith through teaching others. Work in me, and lead me to lasting growth.

You have been believers so long now that you ought to be teaching others. Instead, you need someone to teach you again the basic things about God's word. You are like babies who need milk and cannot eat solid food. HEBREWS 5:12

DAY 63 *Prayerful Moment*

A prayer about MODELING VALUES
When I want to be a good example

LORD,
Everyone models their values by how they spend time, money, and emotions. I profess you as first in my life, but do my actions show that? Help me, Lord, to model what is important to you—your values. I want to influence people the right way, to move them toward Jesus.

Everything else is worthless when compared with the infinite value of knowing Christ Jesus my Lord.
PHILIPPIANS 3:8

DAY 64

A prayer about QUALITY TIME
When relationships matter

TRIUNE GOD,
You have blessed me with wonderful relationships: family and friends who love me and neighbors, coworkers, and others who care about me. What a gift! Thank you. I don't want to take these people for granted; yet often I breeze in and out of their lives without so much as a thought about how we are spending our time together. I know that the problem can be "quantity time"; that is, we need to be together more, and often I let other concerns and events get in the way. People are much more important than that. But I confess that even when I am with a loved one, I am sometimes only there physically; my mind and attention are occupied elsewhere. Even with strangers that is not the way I should act, for each one is your image-bearing, unique creation, whom you love. Help me, instead, Lord, to treat people as individuals, with respect, focusing on them and their needs and not my own, listening, and discussing the important issues of life, not just the superficial. These people and relationships matter.

Love each other with genuine affection, and take delight in honoring each other. ROMANS 12:10

A prayer about TRANSFORMATION
When I need an extreme makeover

HOLY SPIRIT,

I have read the verse for today dozens of times, usually in the context of being different from the world. But at my latest reading, two words jumped out: *let God*. The clear implication is that you don't force yourself on me but wait until you have my permission to change me. In effect, you are saying to me, "Your will be done." That's pretty amazing because the contrast could not be greater. I am nothing, and you are everything, with all power and authority; yet I have this opportunity to *allow* you to transform me. You have a "good and pleasing and perfect" will for me to enjoy, but I can only know and experience it as you change me. And that can happen only as I submit to you and your holy work. The transformation begins with my outlook on life—the way I think. Thank you, Lord, for loving me enough to want to change me and for partnering with me in the process. I definitely need a makeover. So I pray, "Your will be done in me."

Don't copy the behavior and customs of this world, but let God transform you into a new person by changing the way you think. Then you will learn to know God's will for you, which is good and pleasing and perfect. ROMANS 12:2

DAY 66

A prayer about ETERNAL LIFE
When I understand my new life in Christ

SPIRIT OF GOD,

When I first trusted Christ as Savior, I passed from death into life. Before that, not only was I mortal and sentenced to a physical death; I was also dead spiritually and headed for judgment. Then, at my conversion, you took up residence in me and gave me new life, beginning at that moment and lasting forever. Eternal life began then for me and will extend after my time on earth has ended. Some believe that this life is all there is, so when we die, that's it. Others speak of "living on," but they mean in other people's memories. I know the truth—that we were made for eternity. For believers, that means living eternally with you. Everything in the world is temporary, lasting such a short time, and each passing day I am reminded of that truth in my own mind and body. Even though I am grateful for every moment I have to live here for you, I know that my hope is not in this place, in this life, but with you for eternity. Hallelujah!

[Jesus said,] "I tell you the truth, those who listen to my message and believe in God who sent me have eternal life. They will never be condemned for their sins, but they have already passed from death into life." JOHN 5:24

DAY 67

A prayer about MENTORING
When I think about the next generation of believers

DEAR GOD,
Paul's admonition to Timothy hits me hard. Sentenced and imprisoned, Paul knew he would soon be executed by the Romans. Yet instead of feeling sorry for himself, he wrote to his son in the faith, Timothy, giving him encouragement and instructions. Paul knew that the spread of the gospel would depend on the faithfulness of the next generation. So he challenged Timothy to teach to others what he had learned. He also told Timothy to teach his protégés how to "pass [those teachings] on to others." Timothy had a strong mentor, Paul. But he also had the responsibility to come alongside younger believers in a mentoring relationship. I see myself in the role of Timothy, Lord. I need a "Paul" to mentor me, teaching me how to apply your Word to real-life situations. Please lead me to a faithful servant of Christ who is older and wiser and who will work with me. And lead me to those whom I can mentor, I pray. I want to help build up the next generation of believers.

You have heard me teach things that have been confirmed by many reliable witnesses. Now teach these truths to other trustworthy people who will be able to pass them on to others. 2 TIMOTHY 2:2

DAY 68

A prayer about RUNNING THE RACE
When I head for the finish line

MY SAVIOR,
Oh, what a race I am running! When I was much younger, I thought I could run life's race easily and forever. But the racecourse had many unexpected twists, turns, elbows, and obstacles, and now I ache and my energy is waning. I confess that at times I have made life difficult as I struggled to carry burdens as I ran—guilt, anxiety, fear. Forgive me for not giving them to you and for often running with untied shoes, sins that tripped me. Seeing what you endured helps me push through the pain. I am also thankful for the "huge crowd of witnesses" who have finished life's marathon victorious and now enjoy their rewards in heaven with you. What a great encouragement knowing that if they could make it, so can I. Thank you for this faith legacy. In large part, because of their faithfulness I know you. I want to run this life race *for* you and *with* you. I'm in for the duration, so please give me strength and resolve to run well and finish strong.

Since we are surrounded by such a huge crowd of witnesses to the life of faith, let us strip off every weight that slows us down, especially the sin that so easily trips us up. And let us run with endurance the race God has set before us.
HEBREWS 12:1

DAY 69 *Prayerful Moment*

A prayer about PLEASURE
When I exult in God's presence and enjoy his gifts

LOVING FATHER,
My genuinely pleasurable moments come when I enjoy your gifts: family, friends, beauty in nature, and more. I enjoy basking in your presence, fully knowing and feeling who you are and what you have done for me. Thank you, gracious Lord. All these earthly pleasures are just a taste of what's to come in heaven. I can hardly wait!

You will show me the way of life, granting me the joy of your presence and the pleasures of living with you forever.
PSALM 16:11

DAY 70 *Prayerful Moment*

A prayer about HURTS
When I feel wounded

FATHER,
I'm hurting, wounded by a friend. I know no one is perfect, but this caught me by surprise. The words cut deep, and I feel humiliated and betrayed. I don't know what to do or say, how to react. Please show me, lead me—give me the courage to turn the other cheek, to return good for evil, to forgive, to love. And whatever the cause, be with my friend, and do your heart work in both of us.

God called you to do good, even if it means suffering, just as Christ suffered for you. He is your example, and you must follow in his steps. 1 PETER 2:21

DAY 71

A prayer about JESUS
When I look again at the Savior

MY LORD AND MY SAVIOR,

As a child, I thought "Jesus" was your first name and "Christ" your last name. Now I know that *Christ* is the Greek form of "Messiah" or "anointed one," the Person for whom the Jews had longed through the centuries. And the name *Jesus* means "One Who Saves." John's Gospel reveals that you are Creator—the Lord of the universe, of the earth, of your people, and of me. But more than being the Ruler, you are the Savior. You became a living, breathing human being—one of us, with the distinct purpose of saving your people from their sins. I am one of those people, Jesus—not by birth, nationality, or any work or achievement of my own—but completely by your grace. When I was totally dead and lost in my sins, you gave me life—eternal life—forgave me, and saved me. After living a perfect life on earth, you became sin and paid the penalty, dying in my place. But you rose from the dead, defeating death and sin. Thank you, my Lord and my Savior, Jesus Christ.

[Mary] will have a son, and you are to name him Jesus, for he will save his people from their sins. MATTHEW 1:21

DAY 72

A prayer about ESCAPE
When I feel like running away

LOVING FATHER,
Every day brings a variety of challenges, some simple and easy and others complex and difficult. Many involve potential conflicts in relationships; others center on mistakes I've made and must admit. Sometimes I feel like running away from these problems, hiding, closing my eyes, as though by not seeing them I can make them disappear. I act like a small child playing hide-and-seek, assuming that because I can't see anyone, they can't see me. I guess avoiding personal conflicts and dilemmas is a natural reaction—flight rather than fight, and I want to escape. That doesn't help, of course, because the problems remain, waiting for me. I need to confront the issues, so please give me courage and strength. But I know that I won't be alone. You are my hiding place. Wherever I am and whatever I am facing, you are with me, my refuge and my strength. As my refuge, you protect and shelter, and as my strength you empower. I need you. Please help me face my problems and meet them head on . . . with you.

God is our refuge and strength, always ready to help in times of trouble. PSALM 46:1

A prayer about SLEEP
When I prepare to go to bed

DEAR LORD,
I remember as a child praying, "Now I lay me down to sleep; I pray the Lord my soul to keep. If I should die before I wake, I pray the Lord my soul to take." The theology is questionable, but the sentiment is right—trusting you for the soul's safety and destination. As an adult, I have a much clearer understanding of who you are: all powerful—you certainly can keep me secure; all knowing—nothing takes you by surprise; all loving—you love me, want the best for me, and will keep your promise to take me home. Knowing these truths about you, actually knowing *you*, eases the tension of the day, calms my anxious and fearful heart, and gives me peace. Because of my trust in you, I don't have to allow potential problems and conflicts to disturb my sleep. And most important, I know my eternal destiny has been decided because I am your child. Thank you, Lord, for your presence and care. I am safe in your arms. Now I lay me down to sleep.

"I have given rest to the weary and joy to the sorrowing." At this, I woke up and looked around. My sleep had been very sweet. JEREMIAH 31:25-26

A prayer about LISTENING TO OTHERS

When I need to focus my attention and open my ears

SAVIOR,

I get frustrated with those individuals who don't listen to me in a conversation, even when I think I have their full attention. They may become distracted and even look away while I'm talking. Or they may interrupt my story with one of their own or go off on a tangent to what we are discussing. Sometimes they seem to be listening, but in their response, I quickly discover that they haven't heard a word I have said. But you've shown me that I am often like that in my personal interactions. I don't actually listen but am thinking of myself and my needs. I don't want to be that kind of person. Listening is the language of love; it demonstrates concern for others. Help me to be a good listener, Lord. Please keep reminding me when I fall short. Focus my attention on the other person and what he or she is saying. And keep me from pretending to listen while formulating my response. I want to be known as someone who really cares, someone like you.

Understand this, my dear brothers and sisters: You must all be quick to listen, slow to speak, and slow to get angry.

JAMES 1:19

DAY 75

A prayer about SEIZING THE DAY
When I need to make the most of the time I have left

DEAR LORD,
Life is so short. That reality hits me with every passing year, especially when I approach a birthday number that ends with a zero. I want my remaining years to count for you, God. People talk about having a "bucket list," achievements and adventures they want to accomplish and experience before they die. I need a spiritual bucket list, Lord. You said, "The night is coming," and we don't know how much time is left—for anyone. I want to seize the day to make an impact for you. This means sharing with a dear friend the story of my spiritual journey. I have been putting that off. It means going on the short-term mission trip that I've been considering. I also want to give a significant financial contribution to a ministry that is close to my heart; this will involve saving and sacrifice. And I need to step up to a leadership role in church. I know that I can do this only with your blessing and power, and I want to do all for your glory.

We must quickly carry out the tasks assigned us by the one who sent us. The night is coming, and then no one can work.
JOHN 9:4

DAY 76 *Prayerful Moment*

A prayer about PERFECTION
When I feel frustrated in this less-than-perfect world

LORD,
Too often I become dismayed at the flaws I see in myself and others. I know in my mind that you alone are perfect, but help me understand and feel that in my heart. In heaven all will be made whole, right, and perfect. Until then, help me live with a realistic view of the world.

I don't mean to say that I have already achieved these things or that I have already reached perfection. But I press on to possess that perfection for which Christ Jesus first possessed me.
PHILIPPIANS 3:12

DAY 77 *Prayerful Moment*

A prayer about GROWTH
When my faith needs to develop

HOLY SPIRIT,
I feel as though I'm still a baby Christian. I see mature believers who know much about the Bible and theology. Others haven't followed you long, yet their faith seems strong. When I first believed, I enthusiastically read the Bible and shared my faith. Lately, not so much. Lead me to someone who can mentor me in the faith. Rekindle my desire to spend time with you. Help me grow up.

Like newborn babies, you must crave pure spiritual milk so that you will grow into a full experience of salvation. Cry out for this nourishment. 1 PETER 2:2

A prayer about CONTROLLING THE TONGUE
When I say what I shouldn't

FATHER,

I blew it today—my tongue, my words, and my tone of voice got me in trouble again. I had opinions on everything and couldn't shut my mouth. And when others were speaking, I wasn't really listening—I was formulating my answers while waiting for my chance to speak. Then, in a disagreement, instead of keeping quiet and presenting my side with a measured, thoughtful response, I lost my cool and blurted caustic, hateful words that served no purpose except to give me a measure of perverse satisfaction. My expressions were intended to wound, and they succeeded. I'm disciplined in so many areas, but not this one. Why do I have such a difficult time keeping my mouth shut or at least, speaking positively instead of negatively? I am so weak. Forgive me, Lord, for not honoring you in my speech. I want to be different, to care more about the other person than about winning an argument. Above all, I want to care for you. Control my thoughts, feelings, and voice. May my words reflect your work in my life.

The tongue is a small thing that makes grand speeches. But a tiny spark can set a great forest on fire. . . . People can tame all kinds of animals, birds, reptiles, and fish, but no one can tame the tongue. It is restless and evil, full of deadly poison. Sometimes it praises our Lord and Father, and sometimes it curses those who have been made in the image of God.

JAMES 3:5, 7-9

DAY 79

A prayer about MAKING PROGRESS

When I consider God's transforming work in my life

FATHER,

When I gave my life to Christ, that signaled the end of a long journey. I had been living apart from you and was tired of running, and you sought me, found me, and brought me home. But that was also the beginning of another journey—my life together with you. Since then you have been working in me, day by day, little by little, transforming me more and more into the image of your Son. I know I am far from that goal. The process will continue until I see Jesus face to face. But I'm making progress. Some of your lessons have been more difficult than others. And some I've had to learn more than once. Often I seem to take two steps forward but then one step back. Forgive me, Lord, for not listening, not learning, and not trusting. I want to continue to make progress, to grow in my faith. I know that my salvation is secure, that I am safe in your hands, but I don't want to accept the status quo.

We are already God's children, but he has not yet shown us what we will be like when Christ appears. But we do know that we will be like him, for we will see him as he really is. And all who have this eager expectation will keep themselves pure, just as he is pure. 1 JOHN 3:2-3

DAY 80

A prayer about WORDS THAT HEAL
When I think about what I say

DEAR JESUS,
Your ministry was filled with words. You called disciples, taught crowds, rebuked the raging storm, and confronted religious hypocrites. You also spoke to heal the sick and the lame, to cast out demons, and to raise the dead. Words can be powerful, and I want to use mine the right way. I enjoy compliments. Those affirming words lift my spirit and draw me closer to the person giving them. Verbal encouragements have a similar effect. I confess that I do not always use this power righteously. My sinful tendency is to use words as weapons, trying to wound the object of my speech. I do to others what I *do not* want done to me. I need to hold my tongue and to speak healing words. That may mean a compliment or encouragement. It also could be an apology, to help mend a relationship. For that I need courage. Or it could be a verbal acknowledgment of someone's pain, empathizing with the person and praying for him or her. For that I need sensitivity. Please help me use words that heal.

Some people make cutting remarks, but the words of the wise bring healing. PROVERBS 12:18

DAY 81

A prayer about GOVERNMENT
When I question my civil leaders

SOVEREIGN GOD,

Like most people, I complain about the government and my elected representatives—local, state, and national. And in the last general election, many of the candidates I supported lost. So I have been quick to bad-mouth the current political leaders. Your Word clearly states, however, that I should give honor and respect to those who are in authority. What's more, I should *pray* for them! Please forgive me for being so disrespectful, and help me to be a loyal and godly citizen, no matter what my political persuasion. Right now I pray for the president, the vice president, the cabinet, my senators and congressional representatives, the supreme court justices, my governor and other state officials, and my mayor and city officials. I pray that they will trust in you, that you will keep them from harm and corruption, and that they will govern well. Bless their families, too. Thank you for allowing me to live in a country where I can express my faith openly, without fear. I want to be a good citizen and, in so doing, bring glory to your name.

Everyone must submit to governing authorities. For all authority comes from God, and those in positions of authority have been placed there by God. . . . Give respect and honor to those who are in authority. ROMANS 13:1, 7

A prayer about COURAGE
When I feel weak and afraid

MY SAVIOR, MY GOD,
I need you, Lord. I know that you are always with me and working in me, but right now I feel my need for you more than ever. I can't remember a time when I've been this nervous and fearful. I face a challenge like none before, and I'm scared to death of the possible outcome and failure. You know every side of the situation and what I am up against . . . and my fear about the process and potential result. Bolster my spirit and give me clarity of mind and speech. Strengthen my weak legs, I pray, and help me walk forward in faith. My situation isn't close to being as difficult and dire as those faced by Moses, Joshua, and your people approaching Canaan, their Promised Land filled with formidable foes. Yet with your mighty help they succeeded, defeating strong Jericho and a host of enemies. I know you stand with me as well and won't fail me, and I want to trust you. Please give me courage.

Be strong and courageous! Do not be afraid and do not panic before them. For the LORD your God will personally go ahead of you. He will neither fail you nor abandon you.
DEUTERONOMY 31:6

DAY 83 *Prayerful Moment*

A prayer about TENDERNESS
When I act tough

JESUS,
I can act as though nothing gets to me. I behave this way, I guess, to protect myself from others' knowing the real me or from getting hurt. But that tough exterior can get in the way of developing deep relationships and of feeling others' pain. I want to be more like you, Jesus—loving, compassionate, and responsive to others. Please break my heart for what breaks yours.

I will give you a new heart, and I will put a new spirit in you. I will take out your stony, stubborn heart and give you a tender, responsive heart. EZEKIEL 36:26

DAY 84 *Prayerful Moment*

A prayer about TESTING
When I experience trials

FATHER,
The apostle Peter said believers would undergo difficult trials to test their faith. In fact, the early Christians were prepared and purified by terrible persecution. The trials of life are inevitable, so I pray that I meet them with joy and that my faith is shown to be genuine. Burn out the dross and purify me, Lord.

These trials will show that your faith is genuine. It is being tested as fire tests and purifies gold—though your faith is far more precious than mere gold. 1 PETER 1:7

A prayer about PERSPECTIVE
When I need to see from God's point of view

ALMIGHTY GOD,
The other day I was thinking about how children view life. What a limited perspective they have because of their age and their lack of maturity and experience. As they grow older, they discover that the world is much bigger than home, neighborhood, and community. During the school years, they learn about history, geography, nations, and cultures. As an educated, experienced adult with a much larger picture, I can get the idea that I know it all. But even greater than the contrast between a baby's view and mine is the gulf between my perspective and yours, Father. You know everything about everything—the beginning, the end, and the in-between. You know your plans for all of creation, me included, and you see how everything in your plan works together. O Lord, please keep me from pride in my knowledge and opinions. I need to trust fully in you, knowing that you are sovereign, good, and loving. Please help me see life, others, and myself from your point of view as revealed in Scripture. I walk by faith, not by sight.

We have stopped evaluating others from a human point of view. At one time we thought of Christ merely from a human point of view. How differently we know him now!
2 CORINTHIANS 5:16

DAY 86

A prayer about RECONCILIATION
When I have a broken relationship

GRACIOUS LORD,

When we were your enemies and far from you—completely lost in sin, breaking your laws, and rejecting your love—you made the move to reconcile us to yourself. The Incarnation was all for us: God becoming a flesh-and-blood human being, living a perfect life, dying on the cross in our place, becoming the ultimate and final sacrifice for sin, and rising from the grave. Now, by grace and through faith, I have peace with you. I am forgiven, saved, reconciled, brought close. Because of all you have done for me, how can I possibly allow perceived insults, small irritations, and other issues to separate me from my brothers and sisters in Christ? But too often that is what happens, I'm afraid. I know that is wrong, Lord, and I ask for your forgiveness. I want nothing to come between us. I should be quick to forgive, make the first move, and be reconciled. Show me what I should do to help heal those hurts and mend those broken relationships. I want to be like you.

God was in Christ, reconciling the world to himself, no longer counting people's sins against them. And he gave us this wonderful message of reconciliation.
2 CORINTHIANS 5:19

DAY 87

A prayer about HEALING
When the health of someone I love is at risk

DIVINE HEALER,
When Jesus walked this earth, people brought to him their loved ones who were struggling with physical, emotional, and spiritual challenges, and "he healed them all." I have often wished that you were nearby, Lord, so I could bring my requests to you in person. Today, if I could, I would drive my loved one to you to receive your healing touch and be restored. Forgive my lack of faith. I know, in fact, that you are here and your Spirit is working in me and in the world. I also know you can do anything, including healing wherever needed. So, dear God, I lay my loved one at your feet. You can heal immediately if it's your will, and I pray for that. But if you choose to heal through medicine, I pray that you give the doctors wisdom for a correct diagnosis and the right treatment. I place this all in your hands and trust you for the outcome.

Jesus traveled throughout the region of Galilee, teaching in the synagogues and announcing the Good News about the Kingdom. And he healed every kind of disease and illness. News about him spread as far as Syria, and people soon began bringing to him all who were sick. And whatever their sickness or disease, or if they were demon-possessed or epileptic or paralyzed—he healed them all.
MATTHEW 4:23-24

DAY 88

❁ A prayer about GENEROSITY
When I understand all that I have been given

PRECIOUS SAVIOR,

I call myself "thrifty," conservative with my money and spending, although others might say I'm a tightwad. I look for bargains when I shop and use coupons whenever possible. I also hate wasting anything, but that can mean not giving at all and holding on for dear life. I don't think I love money, but I have to admit that sometimes I can act like a miser. You have told us to be good stewards and to be generous, so please help me loosen the strings on my purse. I want to be known as a giver, not a taker. Every day I am surrounded by needy people. Many I know personally, at church and in my neighborhood. Others I learn about through missionary letters, ministry reports, and financial appeals. I want to be a soft touch for the right causes, doing your work and spreading your Word in the world. You have been so generous, even dying on the cross for me. I want to be like you.

Generous people plan to do what is generous, and they stand firm in their generosity. ISAIAH 32:8

A prayer about SHARING MY FAITH
When I know I must witness

DEAR JESUS,

I am surrounded by people who don't know you, many of whom are my friends. I realize that I should be more explicit about what I believe and urge them to learn about you and the Good News, but life just seems to move quickly, and I say little or nothing. I'm not sure what is holding me back. Maybe subconsciously I don't think I'm a good enough Christian to be telling someone else how to live. Perhaps I'm afraid that our friendship will suffer or that they will ask a question I can't answer. I am convinced that you are the Way, the Truth, and the Life, Jesus. I know I was lost in sin but because of your love and the Cross I am forgiven, free, and heaven bound. So why am I so afraid to tell others my story? Please give me the courage to share my faith, trusting you for the outcome. I would ask for opportunities, but you give those every day. I just need to seize them and tell the truth.

How beautiful on the mountains are the feet of the messenger who brings good news, the good news of peace and salvation, the news that the God of Israel reigns! ISAIAH 52:7

DAY 90 *Prayerful Moment*

A prayer about EVIDENCE
When I want proof

LORD ABOVE,
Some people want spectacular signs that you exist. Others believe in a Creator but aren't sure about Jesus—they want proof that he is God. *I* know because I've seen the evidence, especially your work in *me*. But at times, I catch myself wanting even more confirmation. Help me overcome my unbelief, Lord, and help me lay out the evidence for others, that they might also believe.

Jesus replied, "I have already told you, and you don't believe me. The proof is the work I do in my Father's name."
JOHN 10:25

DAY 91 *Prayerful Moment*

A prayer about EXHAUSTION
When I feel wiped out

MY SAVIOR,
Every step seems to take all my energy as this day winds down. Burdens weigh on my mind and emotions—I feel wiped out, drained, totally exhausted. I am desperate for rest and refreshment. You said that those who are weary should come to you. So I'm doing that right now. I name each of my burdens, turning them over to you. In their place, please put your yoke on me, I pray. I love you, Jesus.

Come to me, all of you who are weary and carry heavy burdens, and I will give you rest. MATTHEW 11:28

DAY 92

A prayer about COMMUNICATION

When I share thoughts, feelings, and ideas with others

HEAVENLY FATHER,

Communication is part and parcel of my life. I want to know what's going on and to share my thoughts, opinions, and ideas. So I talk a lot and spend much of my days in conversation with a wide variety of people in all sorts of situations—on the phone, in the neighborhood, at church, over coffee. I also communicate via e-mails and texts. Often, reflecting on what I have said or written, I question my motives for divulging certain information and my use of words. Sometimes I have been privileged with confidential information, and I feel tempted to break confidences. At other times, I want to pass on the latest rumor or piece of gossip. I also find myself making snide comments about another person—hateful words that sting and hurt. Help me think before I speak or write, dear Father. I want all my words to be pleasing to you. And keep me from giving the wrong nonverbal messages through my body language. I want all I do and say to honor you.

Let your conversation be gracious and attractive so that you will have the right response for everyone. COLOSSIANS 4:6

A prayer about EXPECTATIONS
When I set unrealistic standards

ALMIGHTY GOD,
I tend to be a perfectionist, so I get dismayed in this fallen world and continue to be surprised and frustrated when things break or don't work right, illness strikes, and people let me down. But every person sins, makes mistakes, and fails, a fact I often forget. I also set very high standards for my personal performance. That has served me well as a motivation to succeed in many areas, but it also causes me to be disappointed with myself when I don't meet those standards, which happens often. This affects my relationships, too, because I can be critical of friends, neighbors, relatives, and coworkers when they fall short of my unrealistic expectations. Help me to have a realistic perspective, God, accepting the hard truth about human nature and remembering that only you are perfect. I should still work hard to do my best in this world, but I understand that I will only be complete in the next. I certainly should not expect unbelievers to know and do right—I should point them to Christ.

Everyone has sinned; we all fall short of God's glorious standard. ROMANS 3:23

DAY 94

A prayer about PASSION
When I feel my love for God cooling

GRACIOUS GOD,
Several years have passed since I gave my life to you. Over that time I have read and studied your revealed Scriptures, from Genesis to Revelation, and have attended church regularly for worship, teaching, fellowship, and service. I have shelves of Bible reference tools and Christian books. I have attended seminars and gone on short-term missions trips. And I listen to Christian music and radio. If given a test on Bible knowledge or theology, I'm confident that I would do well because I would know the answers. I love you, Lord, I really do, but I feel lukewarm, even cool, in my faith. I remember when I first trusted Christ as Savior. Filled with joy and excitement, I eagerly shared with anyone who would listen about my new relationship with you. What happened? What extinguished that fire? O Lord, "restore to me the joy of your salvation," my passion for you and your Word. I don't want to be a statistic, an average Christian who simply goes through the spiritual motions. I want to be fired up for you.

Restore to me the joy of your salvation, and make me willing to obey you. PSALM 51:12

DAY 95

A prayer about OBEDIENCE
When I analyze my actions

MY LORD AND MY GOD,
I read the story of Samuel confronting King Saul after Israel's victory over the Amalekites. Saul had disobeyed God's direct command and rationalized his actions with words about making sacrifices to you. Saul had it all—power, prestige, and your blessing, but he lost everything. Here he totally missed the point and thought that going through religious motions could take care of his sin. It seems obvious that it couldn't, but I wonder if I ever do that. At times I think that if I go to church more, toss more in the offering, or even read the Bible more, you will think better of me, simply because I am "sacrificing" for you. But you want my heart. And when my heart is right, I will read your Word, listen for your voice, and wholeheartedly obey your commands. Keep me from superficial obedience, Lord. I don't want to be a hypocrite, a phony follower. I want to love you with all of my being and to live as you want me to in every area of life.

Samuel replied, "What is more pleasing to the LORD: your burnt offerings and sacrifices or your obedience to his voice? Listen! Obedience is better than sacrifice, and submission is better than offering the fat of rams." 1 SAMUEL 15:22

DAY 96

A prayer about COMPARISONS
When I measure myself against others

DEAR GOD,

Comparisons can be deadly, but making them can become a habit. In society, people are always being recognized and rewarded for doing better or more than anyone else. The best in sports, singing, dancing, or just being beautiful or handsome are crowned. Today I fell into the comparison trap when I began to excuse my behavior because someone else acted poorly. *I'm so much better*, I thought, and I didn't even consider my own faults and mistakes. At other times I feel bad about myself and my performance because a friend seems to be doing so much better. These are false measurements that can only hurt me, causing me to think that I am either better than I am or worse. I know that your standards and expectations for me are all that matter, that you motivate and empower me through your Spirit to make the right choices, and that you give me grace. Forgive me for these frivolous and worthless comparisons, either excusing or accusing, and help me keep focused on you and your Word.

Pay careful attention to your own work, for then you will get the satisfaction of a job well done, and you won't need to compare yourself to anyone else. For we are each responsible for our own conduct. GALATIANS 6:4-5

DAY 97 *Prayerful Moment*

A prayer about KING JESUS
When I understand Christ's full identity

SAVIOR,
At Christmas we celebrate your birth—a cause for great rejoicing. A few months later, we commemorate Good Friday, a somber time of reflection on your crucifixion. But you rose triumphant and will return as the conquering King. Often I picture you as that infant, but I should remember that you are the almighty King of the universe . . . and my life. Come soon, Lord Jesus.

At just the right time Christ will be revealed from heaven by the blessed and only almighty God, the King of all kings and Lord of all lords. 1 TIMOTHY 6:15

DAY 98 *Prayerful Moment*

A prayer about ENVY
When I resent others for what they have

SOVEREIGN GOD,
To be honest, today I felt unsatisfied with my station in life. Not that I have it so bad, but then I saw what a couple of others had accumulated and accomplished. I became frustrated and felt cheated. The four-letter word for this condition is *envy*—and it's sin. Forgive me, Lord. I am so grateful for what you've given me.

Don't worry about the wicked or envy those who do wrong. . . . Take delight in the LORD, and he will give you your heart's desires. PSALM 37:1, 4

DAY 99

A prayer about DREAMS AND NIGHTMARES
When I lie down to sleep

DIVINE COMFORTER,
Lately I've had trouble falling asleep, regardless of when I go to bed. Then I've tossed and turned all night, sleeping in fits and starts with anxiety-filled, headache-producing dreams. So I'd get up, walk unsteadily to the bathroom, pop in some pain reliever, get ready, and make my way through the day, a little groggy but moving. I'm not sure of the source of these sleep problems. At first I thought the cause was the TV show I had just seen or the snack I had consumed before turning in. But without those, even with no TV or food, the dreams persist. So perhaps the underlying problem is a host of worries, daily stress, relationship issues, a specific fear, or general anxiety. Whatever the reason, I need your comforting presence; I need your peace; I need rest. Please still my conscious and unconscious mind and calm my emotions. And keep my dreams free of nightmares so that I might sleep well and wake up rested and in a good place physically and emotionally, ready to serve you another day.

You can go to bed without fear; you will lie down and sleep soundly. PROVERBS 3:24

A prayer about SICKNESS
When I am ill

GREAT PHYSICIAN,
Being sick can be frustrating, and this illness has dragged on for such a long time—with no end in sight. I can't accomplish much; in fact, I don't feel like doing anything. I have the physician's advice and plenty of medicine, and I have been following the doctor's orders. But I don't seem to be getting any better. Help me, Lord. I need your healing touch. I'm not sure what the problem is, and I'm worried. Please give the doctors wisdom and answers, I pray. You are the Great Physician and the God of miracles. When Jesus was on earth, he healed crippled people, lepers, and the blind. He even raised people back to life. And I know of many times that you have answered prayers for the sick—people near and far have been restored. Although I want desperately to be healed completely, more than anything I want you to be glorified through me, whether I'm healthy or sick. And I know my next life with you in heaven will have no sickness or death. Thank you, Lord.

Such a prayer offered in faith will heal the sick, and the Lord will make you well. And if you have committed any sins, you will be forgiven. JAMES 5:15

DAY 101

A prayer about LIVING FOR GOD
When I want to put my faith into practice

HOLY GOD,
Help me live my life for you! I seem to be careful to live like a Christ follower when my pastors, teachers, and mentors are near. That's certainly how I behaved as a child; when Mom or Dad was nearby, I usually did what I was told, at least while they were watching. As an adult, however, I have learned that I have to be self-disciplined and take responsibility for my actions. The same is true in the spiritual area—my relationship with you. I know that the true test of my faith is when I am on my own, away from my spiritual parents. I take this matter seriously, Lord, and I'm working at it, trying to obey you "with deep reverence and fear." But I know, thankfully, that it's not all up to me—you are working in me, beginning with my desires—helping me *want* to obey you. Then you give me the strength, empowering me to do what you want. Together we move forward in life as I do what pleases you.

Dear friends, you always followed my instructions when I was with you. And now that I am away, it is even more important. Work hard to show the results of your salvation, obeying God with deep reverence and fear. For God is working in you, giving you the desire and the power to do what pleases him. PHILIPPIANS 2:12-13

DAY 102

A prayer about PEACE
When turmoil engulfs me

MY GREAT SHEPHERD,
I feel as though I am at war these days, with bullets flying and chaos reigning. I'm not in great danger or under attack—not fearful for my safety or health—except, perhaps, mental and emotional. But life has become hectic. People are counting on me, so I feel obligated to come through for them. Add to that my regular responsibilities, and I'm always thinking of goals I should reach and tasks I should perform, often for church or another good cause. I need shelter in this storm, a refuge—I need rest and peace. Jesus, in your last words to your disciples, you promised to leave them with the gift of "peace of mind and heart." You knew all the opposition and turmoil they would face and their doubts, questions, and fears. But in the middle of it all, they could have peace—calmness and serenity, knowing that you were in charge. Thank you for that promise to them and to me. Right now I ask for a sense of your presence and the calming assurance that all will be well.

I am leaving you with a gift—peace of mind and heart. And the peace I give is a gift the world cannot give. So don't be troubled or afraid. JOHN 14:27

A prayer about EVERYTHING NEW
When I am feeling old

DEAR GOD,
I know I'm getting older every day—that's how life works. But I felt *old* today. Nothing serious or dramatic happened. I just had some new aches and a fleeting remembrance of an earlier time when life seemed less dramatic and complex. I also remembered being much happier and more hopeful back then. Suddenly I felt as though life was passing me by, and I found myself almost wishing I could reverse the clock, go back to my younger years. Maybe I'm just afraid of what lies ahead—life isn't easy and seems to be getting tougher. Then I read your promise that you are "making everything new." New heavens, new earth, new body—everything restored and relationships renewed. This means no matter how old I am or how I feel and regardless of my problems, pains, and challenges, you are at work in me and around me, making *everything* (including me) brand new. Help me cling to this promise and keep my focus on you and your ultimate and wonderful plan for me.

The one sitting on the throne said, "Look, I am making everything new!" And then he said to me, "Write this down, for what I tell you is trustworthy and true."
REVELATION 21:5

DAY 104 *Prayerful Moment*

A prayer about LASTING
When I'm frustrated with impermanence

DEAR LORD,
Everything I own seems to be wearing out or breaking down. The same is true with my body. Daily I become more aware of my mortality, with new aches and pains. Doesn't anything last? You do—you are "from everlasting to everlasting," and you promise that my life will not end at death but will also last for eternity. Why should I trust in the temporal when I have the eternal one? O Lord, I trust in you.

Praise the LORD, the God of Israel, who lives from everlasting to everlasting. Amen and amen! PSALM 41:13

DAY 105 *Prayerful Moment*

A prayer about BUSYNESS
When my daily schedule is packed

FATHER,
From first light to right now, I have barely had time to breathe. Tomorrow's schedule seems the same—and the next day and the next. Most of what occupies my time is important and good, but I often wonder if I am just running in place. Help me to put my hope in you and your plan, Father. I want to glorify you in all that I do.

We are merely moving shadows, and all our busy rushing ends in nothing. . . . And so, LORD, where do I put my hope? My only hope is in you. PSALM 39:6-7

DAY 106

A prayer about COMPASSION
When I see others in need

SPIRIT OF GOD,

Do your life-changing work in me, I pray. Open my eyes and help me to see others as you see them, to be sensitive to the real needs of the people around me. Sometimes the daily routine pushes so hard that I rush right by those who are hurting; at times I don't know what they need. At other times, I'm calloused and don't really care as I think about my own schedule and concerns. That's wrong. Forgive me and open my eyes and ears. And help me act with compassion as well. Someone may need food, shelter, clothing, or medicine, but a person may just need someone to listen, to care, to be a real friend. So that means I should come alongside them, just as you do with me. And Holy Spirit, be close to my suffering brothers and sisters out of my sight, far away in other lands, persecuted and imprisoned for declaring their allegiance to Christ. When they hurt, I hurt. Thank you for uniting us and making us one.

If someone has enough money to live well and sees a brother or sister in need but shows no compassion—how can God's love be in that person? 1 JOHN 3:17

A prayer about HEALTH
When I hear claims about supernatural healing

DEAR GOD,

I read many stories of miracles in Scripture. Jesus responded to requests to heal the blind, lame, deaf, and demon possessed, and even to raise people from the dead. And you empowered the apostles to heal people. I know you can do anything, and at times, you choose to answer prayers by healing people physically and emotionally—but not always. Some religious people claim that miracles like that happen all the time and that your people can be healthy and wealthy if they have enough faith. But why should we expect special treatment, especially considering that all the disciples experienced harassment and violent persecution? They had as much faith as anyone in history, yet their lives were not easy. I want to enjoy good health and will maintain a healthy lifestyle, eating healthy food as a responsible steward of the body you have given me. And I will continue to pray for healing, for myself and others. But regardless of circumstances, I want to trust you, depending totally on you and seeing each breath as a gift.

[People] had come to hear [Jesus] and to be healed of their diseases; and those troubled by evil spirits were healed. Everyone tried to touch him, because healing power went out from him, and he healed everyone. LUKE 6:18-19

DAY 108

A prayer about FORGIVING OTHERS
When I have been wronged

DEAR JESUS,

While repeating the Lord's Prayer recently, your Spirit highlighted the phrase, "Forgive us our sins, as we have forgiven those who sin against us." The little word *as* means, I think, "in the same way." So I'm asking you to forgive me in the way that I forgive—scary thought. But what if I flip that and forgive others the way you forgive me? I admit my tendency to get even or, at least, hold on to my resentment when someone has hurt me. Forgiving without expecting a response costs me the satisfaction of revenge or proving my point. It's tough, and I resist. But you tell me to be generous in forgiving those who sin against me. Then I remember the sin debt you cancelled for me—totally unearned and undeserved. Even on the cross you forgave those who were crucifying you—me included. In light of that boundless love and grace, how can I consider withholding mercy and grace to those who have wronged me? Please help me love others the way you love, Savior. Help me forgive.

Forgive us our sins, as we have forgiven those who sin against us. . . . If you forgive those who sin against you, your heavenly Father will forgive you. But if you refuse to forgive others, your Father will not forgive your sins.
MATTHEW 6:12, 14-15

A prayer about INSPIRATION
When I consider the gift of your Word

HOLY SPIRIT OF GOD,
What a gift the Bible is to the whole world, to your people, and to me. Every year it tops the bestseller list and is now available worldwide in hundreds of languages and thousands of editions. The Holy Bible is God breathed—"inspired." Over many centuries, you chose certain people to faithfully record your messages. Using their unique personalities, life experiences, and gifts, they wrote exactly what you wanted them to write. And you have preserved your written Word through all these years so that I can read, study, understand, and apply it. This is true for all Scripture, all sixty-six books, so I should not ignore any section, book, or part of a book. When I read the Bible, I am often convicted about what I am doing or the way I am going. Then you reveal to me the path I should take. You promise to "equip [your] people to do every good work." I want to be prepared, fully equipped to defeat temptation and sin; to do what is right; and to glorify you.

All Scripture is inspired by God and is useful to teach us what is true and to make us realize what is wrong in our lives. It corrects us when we are wrong and teaches us to do what is right. God uses it to prepare and equip his people to do every good work. 2 TIMOTHY 3:16-17

DAY 110

A prayer about DISAGREEMENTS
When my friend and I don't see eye to eye

SPIRIT OF GOD,
My friend and I know each other very well, having spent so much time together through the years. We have shared much, so we know each other's talents, dreams, values, stresses, deepest fears, hidden weaknesses, and past mistakes and sins. Thus, in the heat of a conflict or disagreement, I am tempted to use that privileged knowledge to bolster my case or as a weapon, to hurt. I did that today, and I'm ashamed. Whether my position is right or wrong, I never should stoop to saying those kinds of things. It's not fair or loving and doesn't reflect Christ in me. I don't want to be the kind of person who lashes out without thinking. People do not always agree; even the closest of friends will have differences of opinion, some strongly held. At those times, help me, Holy Spirit, to keep my cool and to present my side with care for the other person. And especially in this situation, please give me the opportunity and the right words to ask for forgiveness.

Don't use foul or abusive language. Let everything you say be good and helpful, so that your words will be an encouragement to those who hear them.
EPHESIANS 4:29

DAY 111 *Prayerful Moment*

A prayer about PROTECTION
When I am concerned about my safety

LORD GOD,
I am trusting you with my well-being. I know that when I follow you and am in your will, you protect me from injury and death unless they are for the best. At times I have been in situations where I was nervous and afraid, almost fearful for my life. And you brought me safely through. Thank you, dear Lord. My life is in your hands.

God's way is perfect. All the LORD's promises prove true. He is a shield for all who look to him for protection.
2 SAMUEL 22:31

DAY 112 *Prayerful Moment*

A prayer about GOD'S CARE
When I feel burdened and alone

MY FATHER,
I know you care *about* me; you loved me so much that you sent Jesus to die for me. But you also care *for* me, as a loving Father for his child. This means that you are with me always, watching, guarding, and guiding. Recently I've felt weighed down by concerns for myself and others. And I wonder why I have so little faith. I want to trust you more, so right now, I give you all my worries and cares. Thank you for carrying this load for me.

Give all your worries and cares to God, for he cares about you.
1 PETER 5:7

DAY 113

A prayer about DISCERNMENT

When I need heavenly wisdom

GRACIOUS GOD,

I need your wisdom, always. Whenever I trust only in my own thoughts and ideas, I complicate matters and, at times, even head into disaster. Every day I am confronted with questions in various areas of life—relationships, investment of money and time, work, and others. These issues concern whether something is true or not, whom I can trust, the direction I should take. This week—today, in fact—several paths lie before me, and I need to choose just one. They all look right; they all seem good. Relying completely on myself, my own thoughts and emotions, I tend to rationalize or feel my way along. Instead I need to discern your will. I know that begins by carefully studying your Word, rightly interpreting it, and personally applying it. So I ask you to please give me discernment to understand your Word. Then, when I know what you want me to believe and do, give me the courage and strength to follow through.

Give discernment to me, your servant; then I will understand your laws. PSALM 119:125

A prayer about MOTIVES

When I want to be sure I do what is right for the right reasons

DEAR JESUS,

I want to do what is right in all areas of my life—physical, mental, social, and spiritual. But I need to act for the right reasons. Sometimes, regardless of what I profess, I talk in a certain way to make a good impression on others, even when participating in a Bible study or Sunday school class. At times, I may try to enhance my reputation when I feed those who are hungry, serve the needy, or do another act of kindness. I may even give money to the church to gain some sort of recognition or influence. And often I act out of guilt. All those motives fall woefully short of what you want, and some are sinful. When I do good works for self-serving reasons, I harm my relationship with you and rob myself of the joy you want me to have. Please forgive me, Lord. Purify my heart. I want to do everything for the Kingdom with the goal of bringing glory to you. May my actions flow from my love and gratitude for you.

People may be pure in their own eyes, but the LORD examines their motives. PROVERBS 16:2

DAY 115

A prayer about TRUST IN GOD
When I consider the level of my faith

HEAVENLY FATHER,

My money bears the inscription "In God We Trust," but as a nation we mostly trust our army, stock market, government, and businesses. So the phrase has lost much of its original meaning. I also claim to trust in you, but I wonder if I really do or if the term has become simply a cliché. Is my trust in you such that if, like Job, I lost everything I could still say, "God might kill me, but I have no other hope"? I *know* you are my only hope in this life and the next, but I'm not sure I act that way. I tend to lean greatly on people who love me—family and friends. So I wonder whether I could survive with only you with me. And I think I look to my job and finances for security. How would I respond if I suddenly became destitute? Trusting in you fully means believing that you love me and want only the best for me. I do believe that, Father. I do.

God might kill me, but I have no other hope. JOB 13:15

A prayer about DEFEAT
When I suffer a setback

AWESOME GOD,

You never promised that life would be smooth sailing, and today I hit some rough seas. I was moving along in the right direction with my goal in sight when, wham! I was stopped in my tracks. The setback left me feeling down, totally defeated. Perhaps my expectations, my goals, were too high, ot I may have been too idealistic, assuming the best-case scenario. In any event, things didn't turn out that way, and I fell short. I crashed, I lost—and now I have to start over. But you are so much bigger than my situation, my defeat; you are sovereign, in control of everything. I need to remember that always, especially in times like these. You will have the ultimate victory. Help me to keep my head up and start fresh tomorrow morning, focused on you and your loving plan. Please give me the picture of where I should start, what my first steps should be. I want to believe, to feel in my soul, that this will work out. I want to trust you fully.

We are pressed on every side by troubles, but we are not crushed. We are perplexed, but not driven to despair. We are hunted down, but never abandoned by God. We get knocked down, but we are not destroyed.
2 CORINTHIANS 4:8-9

A prayer about UNITY
When I see divisions in the church

DEAR LORD,

Clearly you want your people to be unified, to be one—I find this stated often in Scripture. But the church has been anything but that in our two thousand years of history, with schisms, trials, and even wars. In my lifetime, I've heard of or witnessed several church splits. Occasionally theology is the dividing issue, sometimes rightly so. But usually the offense comes from a new worship style, a beloved staff member being dismissed, the way the youth ministry uses a building, or even the color of the carpet in the new addition. I feel th is deeply right now because a few members in my church are stirring things up, trying to move against the pastor. What they are doing is wrong and certainly not how your people should behave. Please bring these individuals to their spiritual senses. I pray *against* Satan, bitterness, and anger, and I pray *for* understanding, healing, and love. And show me how I can be a peacemaker here. Unify your church—locally, nationally, and internationally—around our Savior and our common mission. Make us one.

[Jesus said,] "I am praying not only for these disciples but also for all who will ever believe in me through their message. I pray that they will all be one, just as you and I are one—as you are in me, Father, and I am in you. And may they be in us so that the world will believe you sent me."

JOHN 17:20-21

DAY 118 *Prayerful Moment*

A prayer about LIMITATIONS
When I realize I can't do it all

DEAR FATHER,
I sometimes actually believe I can solve just about every problem and interpersonal conflict. But I can't. So I turn to you, admitting my weakness and frailty. I know that you want me to use the resources you've entrusted to me for your glory, but you don't expect me to do that alone or in my own strength. Please do your work, limitless God.

All glory to God, who is able, through his mighty power at work within us, to accomplish infinitely more than we might ask or think. EPHESIANS 3:20

DAY 119 *Prayerful Moment*

A prayer about LORDSHIP
When I need to remember who's in charge

CHRIST MY SAVIOR,
I call you Lord, and I really mean it. But sometimes I forget what that title implies. You are in charge of my life, calling all the shots. Forgive me for acting as though I know better than you. John the Baptist told his followers, "[Jesus] must become greater . . . , and I must become less." John could have felt threatened by your influence and authority, but he knew you were his Savior and God's Son. May I have that same attitude, I pray.

He must become greater and greater, and I must become less and less. JOHN 3:30

DAY 120

A prayer about PAIN
When I am suffering

HEAVENLY FATHER,
You know I am hurting. I feel miserable, and the pain is almost unbearable. I want relief, even a brief respite. I know, Lord, that you see and care for me. I am your child, and you love me and want only the best for me. So what I am going through is in your plan—it didn't catch you by surprise. And I am certain that I should be learning from this experience—perseverance, patience, compassion for others in a similar condition, or another valuable life lesson. But God, I need you now. Show me what I should do, what medicine to take. Give the doctor wisdom. And please help me get good sleep tonight and wake up refreshed and able to think clearly. I get so frustrated with my mortality. I eagerly anticipate the day when I will be freed from my weak and frail flesh that is subject to sickness and death, when I will be delivered from this sinful world and will be with you in heaven, totally released, with a new body. Thank you for that glorious promise.

We believers also groan, even though we have the Holy Spirit within us as a foretaste of future glory, for we long for our bodies to be released from sin and suffering. We, too, wait with eager hope for the day when God will give us our full rights as his adopted children, including the new bodies he has promised us. ROMANS 8:23

A prayer about ENERGY
When I need God's power

HOLY SPIRIT,

You indwell Christ followers, transforming us and infusing us with power to resist temptation, deal with sinful habits, serve others, and spread the Good News about Jesus. I can do none of that in my strength, on my own. Whenever I try—even with great effort—I fall short, I fail. Because all I do for you has to be you working through me. The world, *my* world, is filled with people heading in the wrong direction. Some have heard of Jesus and may have read select Bible stories, but most have no idea of the gospel tenets. Today my path crossed those of several friends and associates who fit that category and with whom I want to share my faith. I love these folks and know that they are lost without Christ. So I pray for them right now, by name, and I ask you to give me opportunities, words, and *power*. Fill me—energize me—to be your spokesperson. I want to help change the world, one person at a time—beginning with me.

[Jesus said,] "You will receive power when the Holy Spirit comes upon you. And you will be my witnesses, telling people about me everywhere—in Jerusalem, throughout Judea, in Samaria, and to the ends of the earth." ACTS 1:8

DAY 122

A prayer about MATERIALISM
When I see the allure of possessions

DEAR LORD,

It feels like an all-out assault. Ubiquitous advertisements urge me to own the latest, greatest, super, advanced, upgraded, cool, and desirable material thing. Whether on the Internet, television, radio, or smart phone, in newspapers and magazines, or on billboards and flyers, I am continually barraged with sales pitches for a wide variety of "must-have" products: cars, phones, clothes, computers/notebooks, home furnishings, appliances, jewelry, tools. I can easily dismiss or ignore many of these plugs, but some get through and pull me in. I know from experience that none of these highly touted things last; they soon decay, rust, break, or become obsolete. Yet still I am tempted, especially when my friends and coworkers show off their latest purchases. Please keep me from materialism, Lord, thinking that the latest gift or purchase will make me happy or fulfilled. I want to keep my priorities straight and to be a good steward, using and spending my resources wisely and for your Kingdom.

Think about the things of heaven, not the things of earth. For you died to this life, and your real life is hidden with Christ in God. And when Christ, who is your life, is revealed to the whole world, you will share in all his glory.
COLOSSIANS 3:2-4

DAY 123

A prayer about KNOWING
When I need assurance

MY GOD AND FATHER,
I know that tough times bring tough questions. My situation certainly is not desperate, just a bit rocky, but lately I have been feeling unsure about my faith and the future. The economy, political developments, world events, and personal stress seem to be bringing me down, especially when I am physically and emotionally tired. In 2 Timothy, however, you remind me of your faithfulness through Paul's powerful example and strong faith. Paul had given everything to take the gospel across the world, but when he wrote this letter, he was sitting in a dank prison hole, abandoned by all but a few friends. He was cold and alone. And Paul understood that this would be his last imprisonment; he was awaiting execution. Yet he still could assert his confidence in you. Knowing you, he could be *sure* of his future, regardless of his present circumstances. My circumstances aren't nearly as difficult, but I need that confident assurance, Lord. Please bolster my faith, I pray, and help me to entrust everything to you.

I am suffering here in prison. But I am not ashamed of it, for I know the one in whom I trust, and I am sure that he is able to guard what I have entrusted to him until the day of his return. 2 TIMOTHY 1:12

A prayer about GOING THE DISTANCE
When I think about life in the long term

GRACIOUS AND LOVING SAVIOR,
In a NASCAR race, often a car will be in the lead and doing well when suddenly a little bump or debris on the track or a driver mistake causes the car to spin out of control and wreck. Unfortunately that's an apt metaphor for life because weekly, it seems, I hear about a public personality following that pattern—out front, traveling fast, doing great . . . but then a crash and burn. I have seen this played out with friends as well. They seem to be doing just fine spiritually, and then they hit a wall. I don't want that to be my story, Lord. I want to run the race, the whole race, and live well for you—as Eugene Peterson says, "a long obedience in the same direction." It's not just a matter of moral failure; sometimes the way is so rough that I feel like quitting. At those times, please give me stamina and determination to continue living your way by your power. No matter what happens, I want to go the distance.

You were running the race so well. Who has held you back from following the truth? GALATIANS 5:7

DAY 125 *Prayerful Moment*

A prayer about RELIANCE
When I begin to trust in my own strength

GOD,
I have been taught to be independent, disciplined, and self-reliant. But I know that my salvation was by grace through faith—my religious efforts meant nothing. I also know that my growth as your follower depends on you. Yet I keep trying to live for Christ on my own. Forgive me, Lord. I want to rely completely on you.

We rely on what Christ Jesus has done for us. We put no confidence in human effort. PHILIPPIANS 3:3

DAY 126 *Prayerful Moment*

A prayer about CONFRONTATION
When I should tell someone an inconvenient truth

GOD,
Someone I care about is making bad decisions. I know I should say something, but I'm afraid of rupturing the relationship. The world says personal lifestyle choices are private, but I know different. My friend professes to be a Christ follower, and your Word speaks clearly in these matters. Prepare my friend's heart to be open to my confrontation. Help me sense the right time to speak up. Please give me the words to say with love.

An open rebuke is better than hidden love! Wounds from a sincere friend are better than many kisses from an enemy.
PROVERBS 27:5-6

A prayer about SEX
When my eyes and thoughts stray

LOVING FATHER,
What a dirty mind I have! Forgive me, I pray, for my impure thoughts and my habit of dwelling on them. You created everything good, including sex—what an incredible gift. Yet Satan has twisted and cheapened this natural urge, leading many astray. Empower me to resist the pull of dirty jokes, pornography, and innuendoes, which focus my lustful thoughts on pleasing myself at the expense of another. You made this drive for procreation, expressing love, and enjoyment but only within marriage, where sex can be fully expressed and enjoyed. Society is littered with unwanted pregnancies, prostitution, scandals, dissolved marriages, and broken promises and lives because people believe the lies about your gift. Popular culture talks of love but makes sex the ultimate pleasure—it's overrated. But it also presents sex as free and easy, with no consequences—undervalued. Free me from this trap, I pray. Show me the way to go in order to flee temptation and then the courage to take the better way. Purify me in mind and body for your sake.

God's will is for you to be holy, so stay away from all sexual sin. Then each of you will control his own body and live in holiness and honor—not in lustful passion like the pagans who do not know God and his ways.
1 THESSALONIANS 4:3-5

A prayer about WORK
When I know my labor matters to God

HEAVENLY FATHER,
At every place of employment, virtually all employees seem to view work as a necessary evil. They live for breaks, quitting time, and weekends. I don't want to have that attitude, but I feel as though I am slipping into it, using my work simply as a means to an end, for the money. That's terrible stewardship because my job comprises more than a third of every day! I know that work isn't bad, because you gave Adam an assignment *before* sin entered the world. But I also understand that not all work is good—I shouldn't do anything that violates your commands or causes others to do so. Please help me find meaning and joy in my occupation, and show me how I can do my job in a way that glorifies you. I ask you to guide me to where I can best use the abilities and mind that you gave me. And on the job, may my coworkers see that I am working for you and be drawn to Christ.

Work willingly at whatever you do, as though you were working for the Lord rather than for people.
COLOSSIANS 3:23

DAY 129

A prayer about OPPORTUNITIES

When I choose to seize the moments that God provides

DEAR LORD,

This day, as every day, was a gift. Looking back on the past fourteen hours, I see all your generous gifts during that time: food, transportation, work, laughter, friends, insight, and the ability to perceive and experience all that life offers. But almost hidden among those more obvious gifts were the opportunities you provided. At those times you gave me possibilities and choices. Thank you for that amazing gift. You gave me the chance to act in love and meet someone's need, a time to overlook a slight, and many moments for prayer. I know that in the future you will also give me the opportunity to respond to a hurt with grace, to ignore an insulting remark, to serve, to praise, to teach, to resist temptation, to resolve a conflict, and to share the Good News of salvation. Thank you for allowing me to choose to seize these moments and do what is right and what honors you. Please give me sensitivity and awareness so I don't miss them. I can hardly wait to see tomorrow's opportunities.

Be careful how you live. Don't live like fools, but like those who are wise. Make the most of every opportunity in these evil days. EPHESIANS 5:15-16

DAY 130

A prayer about MY BODY
When I consider my physique

DEAR GOD,

You made me the way I am, and for most of my life I accepted that, especially as a child—I wasn't too concerned about my body. These days, however, I seem to have a love-hate relationship with my physique. Sometimes I like how I look; other times, not so much, especially when I compare myself to the young and fit bodies at the gym. Often I pamper my body and work to keep in shape, making sure to exercise, grab eight hours of sleep, take vitamins and antioxidants, and eat right—fat-free and low calorie. At other times I abuse it, snacking on junk, guzzling coffee, staying up way too late—adding pounds and cholesterol in the process. You created me with my physical makeup—height, basic shape, senses, organs, and limbs. Help me accept the truth that you know me and love me that way. But you have also given me a stewardship responsibility. So please give me the discipline to take care of myself so I can better live and serve. My body is yours.

Don't you realize that your body is the temple of the Holy Spirit, who lives in you and was given to you by God? You do not belong to yourself, for God bought you with a high price. So you must honor God with your body.

I CORINTHIANS 6:19-20

A prayer about GUILT
When I'm feeling remorseful for something I've done

HEAVENLY FATHER,
I was born with a conscience, so I've always had an inner voice telling me when an action was wrong. Since giving my life to you, I also have the Holy Spirit inside me, convicting me of my sin. The urgings of both conscience and the Spirit lead to guilt feelings when I do something I know I shouldn't. And that has helped me confess to you and make good choices. I also know that Satan tries to make me feel guilty when I don't need to. The Accuser twists your Word and reminds me of past mistakes and sins. Lord, I want to listen only to *you*, to obey your commands and follow your guidance. Before Christ, I was lost, dead, completely and totally guilty, and deserving of eternal punishment. But you found me, gave me life, and pronounced me "not guilty." Regardless of what Satan or anyone else might say, I know I am forgiven of all my sin—past, present, and future. Thank you, and please help me live as one who has been reborn, redeemed, and released.

Your sins have been forgiven through Jesus. 1 JOHN 2:12

DAY 132 *Prayerful Moment*

A prayer about ORGANIZATION
When I desire to be more focused and efficient

FATHER,
Normally I'm fairly organized. Lately, however, I've noticed my schedule, car, and desk have become cluttered, and I have succumbed to the tyranny of the urgent. I need to resolve to say no to nonpriority requests. Give me the determination to do what you want and the discipline to toss the stuff that has piled up. Please help me be more organized, focused, and efficient.

God is not a God of disorder but of peace.
1 CORINTHIANS 14:33

DAY 133 *Prayerful Moment*

A prayer about CONFIDENCE
When I feel unsure

SOVEREIGN LORD,
I can be tentative—insecure and afraid. You hold me in your loving hands, so why do I *ever* fail to trust you? I am weak; you are strong. I am finite; you are infinite. My perspective and resources are limited; you see and own everything. I want to live in confidence, knowing that you are with me, sensing your presence. Please give me strength. Help me to boldly live for you.

Only in returning to me and resting in me will you be saved. In quietness and confidence is your strength.
ISAIAH 30:15

A prayer about LONGINGS
When I desire to point others to you

MY GRACIOUS HEAVENLY FATHER,
You created humans in your image, and you put eternity in their hearts. You made them for fellowship with you. So we are incomplete without you. Yet ever since the sin in the Garden, we have tried to live our own way. Pascal said that everyone has a God-shaped vacuum—a hole in the soul that only you can fill. This vacuum is a longing for meaning, for completion, for home. Every day I see people desperately seeking, Lord. Sensing their emptiness, they try filling it with money or experiences or sex or alcohol or relationships or career successes or any number of other things. I want to reach these people for you, Lord. They are my neighbors and coworkers and friends. Father, please make me sensitive to when they hit bottom or I sense that their search has been futile. Give me opportunities to present the truth of the gospel. Jesus is the *only* way to you, and I need to share that in love. Help them to be restless until they rest in you.

God has made everything beautiful for its own time. He has planted eternity in the human heart, but even so, people cannot see the whole scope of God's work from beginning to end. ECCLESIASTES 3:11

DAY 135

A prayer about BLESSINGS
When I consider God's work in my life

O LORD,

The word *blessing* is used often in Scripture and in life in a variety of contexts. In my relationship with you, "blessing" means having your approval and receiving your good gifts. Today was filled with your blessings, beginning with another day to live and serve you. After a night of safe and sound sleep, I awoke, prepared for the day, and made my way through it under your care. Whether showering, eating, reading, walking, working out, thinking, talking, running, sitting, or driving, you were with me. Thank you. I have a place to live, air to breathe, water to drink, and food to eat. Thank you. I was able to experience your glorious creation—sun, sky, earth, flowers, trees, birds, animals, rivers, weather—with my senses. I saw, I heard, I smelled, I touched. Thank you. I have family, friends, neighbors, coworkers, and Christian brothers and sisters who care about me, help me, support me, seek my company, and pray for me. Thank you. And of eternal importance, through Christ I am forgiven, Spirit empowered, and free. Thank you.

All praise to God, the Father of our Lord Jesus Christ, who has blessed us with every spiritual blessing in the heavenly realms because we are united with Christ.

EPHESIANS 1:3

A prayer about RIDICULE
When I laugh at others' mistakes

DEAR LORD,
I'm known as a jokester for my sense of humor. I am always ready with a quick retort or wisecrack—puns, one-liners, clever remarks. This usually helps me build friendships as we laugh together. And my humor can defuse tension and get us through serious moments. But sometimes my quick wit backfires as my mind and tongue get me in trouble. A strength becomes a weakness. I remember ridiculing someone's physical characteristic and, at another time, another person's lack of musical skill. Today I mocked a good friend who had made a careless mistake and looked foolish. In each case, the person was hurt and offended by my thoughtless, caustic comments. I need your help to let me know when to keep my mouth shut and how to respond differently in certain situations. I also need to repair the relationship with my friend, asking for forgiveness. Yes, I still want to have fun and use humor, but I desire more to be seen as someone who is serious about you and sensitive to individuals' feelings, someone who treats people with respect.

Throw out the mocker, and fighting goes, too. Quarrels and insults will disappear. PROVERBS 22:10

DAY 137

A prayer about BEING SPIRIT LED
When I understand God's work in me

SPIRIT OF GOD,
Do your powerful, life-changing work in me, I pray. When I gave my life to Christ, you came into my life; since then, you are constantly transforming me into the kind of person you want and that I should be. You give me new perspective, thoughts, values, and strength. You also give me words to speak and potential actions to take. And you lead me as I submit to your direction and control. At times your leading is obvious to me, at other times much more subtle. But always you are guiding me to opportunities to glorify God by showing compassion, serving, listening, meeting needs, correcting, encouraging, comforting, and telling others about Christ. What a privilege to be used by you! You also tell me what not to do and what to avoid. I am continually amazed at the way you lead and direct. The only problem, however, is that sometimes I don't submit to you, either by ignoring you or choosing to disobey. Please forgive me. Keep me in tune with you, sensitive to your will. Lead me.

Dear brothers and sisters, you have no obligation to do what your sinful nature urges you to do. For if you live by its dictates, you will die. But if through the power of the Spirit you put to death the deeds of your sinful nature, you will live. For all who are led by the Spirit of God are children of God. ROMANS 8:12-14

A prayer about HYPOCRISY
When I see the Pharisee in me

JESUS,

You blasted the teachers of religious law and the Pharisees for being hypocrites because they made a great show of piety while being corrupt and sinful in their hearts. These men had reached a spiritual pinnacle, but it was one of their own making, not one that brought them closer to you. In reality, they were phonies, professing to be holy and devoted but using their religion as a weapon and as a way to gain status. I read the stories of your confrontations with these men in their flowing robes and wonder how they could be so blind to those inconsistencies. Yet I see the same tendencies in me. I can easily compare myself favorably with people who seem less devoted to the church and ministry. And as I scurry around doing spiritual activities, I can begin to believe that I really am "holier than thou." I repent, Lord. I don't want to be like a whitewashed tomb—"beautiful on the outside" but dead on the inside. I want to be your person through and through. Keep my heart pure, my priorities straight, and my eyes off others and on you.

What sorrow awaits you teachers of religious law and you Pharisees. Hypocrites! For you are like whitewashed tombs—beautiful on the outside but filled on the inside with dead people's bones and all sorts of impurity. Outwardly you look like righteous people, but inwardly your hearts are filled with hypocrisy and lawlessness. MATTHEW 23:27-28

DAY 139 *Prayerful Moment*

A prayer about SURRENDER
When I give up and give in

LORD JESUS,
I know I must give you every area of my life, but that is so difficult. Afraid of what might happen, I keep holding on instead of letting go. But you know best and I must trust you. To follow you, I first have to turn completely in your direction, and that's what I want to do. I surrender.

If any of you wants to be my follower, you must turn from your selfish ways, take up your cross, and follow me.
MATTHEW 16:24

DAY 140 *Prayerful Moment*

A prayer about THE SIN NATURE
When I honestly assess myself

GOD,
Ever since Eden, humans having sinful natures have been born into a sinful world. Our natural bent is to turn away from you and your will. So I shouldn't be shocked when people act naturally and sin. I also shouldn't be surprised when *I* act that way, and it should remind me how much I need you. Enslaved by sin, I was lost and without hope. But you freed me from sin's penalty and power. You have given me the freedom to choose to do what is right, to serve you. Thank you, Lord.

I was born a sinner—yes, from the moment my mother conceived me. PSALM 51:5

A prayer about DISAPPOINTMENT
When life doesn't go my way

FATHER,
I remember a childhood experience that shattered my world. When I didn't get what I wanted and expected, I was heartbroken and couldn't be consoled, convinced it was the worst possible thing that could ever happen. Now I see it was no big deal . . . but it was to me at the time. And I remember a few years later feeling the same way in a relationship crisis. Again, I thought I would die, but life went on. Looking back, I can hardly believe the event affected me so much. What a change perspective makes! I need to remember that lesson, Lord, *right now*, in this disappointment. If I could only see life from your point of view, I'd see how you are weaving the tapestry of my life. But at this moment, I am frustrated, angry, and sad. Please dry my tears and heal my broken heart. Help me know that you are watching over me and that this will pass. I need to trust you and keep moving forward.

We can rejoice, too, when we run into problems and trials, for we know that they help us develop endurance. And endurance develops strength of character, and character strengthens our confident hope of salvation. And this hope will not lead to disappointment. For we know how dearly God loves us, because he has given us the Holy Spirit to fill our hearts with his love. ROMANS 5:3-5

DAY 142

A prayer about FAITH AND WORKS
When my efforts for Christ slacken

DEAR LORD,

I am so grateful that my salvation depends totally on you—I am saved by grace alone, through faith alone! I used to be like most people, thinking I could earn your favor and eternal life by regularly attending church, not breaking big commandments, and generally trying to be good. I can remember thinking that my good deeds just had to outweigh my bad ones. That sounds reasonable, but in truth, just one sin is enough to keep me out of heaven. Now I know that in terms of my relationship with you, all those "good deeds" mean nothing. Unfortunately, I can use that truth as an excuse for *not* working out my faith: showing mercy, fighting injustice, stewarding my resources, acting in love, and speaking truth. James says that without good works faith is "dead and useless" in terms of making any impact in the world. Please keep me from becoming complacent or lazy in my faith, Lord. I want to work hard for you, *as a result* of your work in me.

You see, faith by itself isn't enough. Unless it produces good deeds, it is dead and useless. Now someone may argue, "Some people have faith; others have good deeds." But I say, "How can you show me your faith if you don't have good deeds? I will show you my faith by my good deeds."
JAMES 2:17-18

A prayer about GRIEF
When I am overcome with sorrow

O GOD,
I don't know how much more I can take. This loss seems beyond what I can bear, dear Lord. I remember as a child weeping over a favorite toy that was broken. Later, as an adolescent, a shattered romance tore my heart. So I've experienced loss before . . . but never like this—so strong and so deep that I wonder how I can go on. The funeral was hard, but the grief hit hardest as I walked slowly away from the grave. You fully understand my feelings because you experienced the most devastating and profound loss imaginable. So help me now, I pray. O Divine Comforter—heal and comfort my soul. I know death is not final—I know that in my mind, and I truly believe it. So why doesn't that truth translate to my feelings? I want to stop my crying and move on. Please, Lord, give me peace. Let me know you are here, with me at this time. Give me hope and strength to turn the page on this dark chapter of my life.

May our Lord Jesus Christ himself and God our Father, who loved us and by his grace gave us eternal comfort and a wonderful hope, comfort you and strengthen you in every good thing you do and say. 2 THESSALONIANS 2:16-17

DAY 144

A prayer about GOD'S IMAGE
When I think about being created

GOD,

In Genesis I read about your special creation of human beings, beginning with the first two people, a male and a female, Adam and Eve. Those two were quite different from the rest of Creation because you created them in your image. I don't know all that your "image" entails, but I do know that all of us human creatures are somehow like you. I need to remember that profound truth when wondering if I have any value to you. Thank you, Lord, for endowing me with worth and giving me responsibility for caring for planet Earth. But I also need to remember that *all* people are your image bearers—talkative coworkers, annoying neighbors, irritating relatives, opposition politicians, aggressive nonbelievers, and even hardened criminals and terrorists. I can easily write off certain people as "worthless," or at least not worth the effort. Please help me see people of every age, race, nationality, and life station as you see them—valuable and special. And show me how to share your love with them.

God said, "Let us make human beings in our image, to be like us. They will reign over the fish in the sea, the birds in the sky, the livestock, all the wild animals on the earth, and the small animals that scurry along the ground." So God created human beings in his own image. In the image of God he created them; male and female he created them.
GENESIS 1:26-27

DAY 145

A prayer about DOUBTS
When I question my faith

ETERNAL GOD,
"Never doubt in darkness what God has shown you in the light." Today I needed to be reminded of that quote from Dr. V. Raymond Edman because I felt the dark closing in and questions beginning to form at the edges of my faith. This kind of darkness has many forms, among them stress, tragedy, and depression. Today, it was the realization of my lack of resources compared to my obligations. So I felt as though I were standing in a room with no source of light. The longer I stood in the dark, the more susceptible I was to questioning what was actually in the room—because I couldn't see anything. But I know Jesus, the Truth, and I trust your Word. On brighter days, you have revealed much to me. You have chosen, saved, forgiven, and changed me—that I know for sure. And I recall your promises and other mighty deeds on my behalf. Please dismiss my doubts, allay my fears, and strengthen my weak faith. I want to stand strong and move mountains for you.

Jesus told them, "I tell you the truth, if you have faith and don't doubt, you can do things like [the miracle I did] and much more. You can even say to this mountain, 'May you be lifted up and thrown into the sea,' and it will happen. You can pray for anything, and if you have faith, you will receive it." MATTHEW 21:21-22

DAY 146 *Prayerful Moment*

A prayer about LISTENING TO GOD
When I need sensitivity to divine direction

LORD,
Sometimes I wonder how I can be so blind and deaf. Only later when I reflect on a day, week, or month do I see that—through a passage of Scripture, a word from a friend, or an event—you were trying to get my attention. I want to be sensitive to you, Lord. Open my ears, I pray, so I can hear your direction.

I listen carefully to what God the LORD is saying, for he speaks peace to his faithful people. But let them not return to their foolish ways. PSALM 85:8

DAY 147 *Prayerful Moment*

A prayer about LUST
When I begin to crave the things of the world

GOD ABOVE,
Please help me stay focused on you and your will. Too often I find my eyes and mind wandering, and I begin lusting after physical pleasure, money, power, achievements, or possessions. I know those are dead ends. I do not want to love the world, only you—first and foremost.

Do not love this world . . . , for the world offers only a craving for physical pleasure, a craving for everything we see, and pride in our achievements and possessions. These are not from the Father, but are from this world. And this world is fading away. 1 JOHN 2:15-17

DAY 148

A prayer about PREPARATION

When I think about being ready to meet Christ

MY LORD AND SAVIOR,

When you left earth, you promised to return one day when we least expect it. Some people have thought that being ready means waiting patiently—many have even tried to figure out the exact time of your second coming. That's not me, but I can become complacent and even forget that you could come back at any moment. So I want to be prepared for that glorious event. Please show me, Lord, the specifics of preparation for my life. I know that means loosening my grip on this world and all it offers because, in the words of the old chorus, "This world is not my home." It also means taking Spirit-led opportunities to share the Good News in my style, using the gifts you have given to me. And being prepared means living in such a way that I would not be ashamed at your appearing—living as your child and honoring you with my thoughts, words, and deeds. Even so, come Lord Jesus, and please come soon.

I solemnly urge you in the presence of God and Christ Jesus, who will someday judge the living and the dead when he appears to set up his Kingdom: Preach the word of God. Be prepared, whether the time is favorable or not.

2 TIMOTHY 4:1-2

DAY 149

A prayer about THE PERSECUTED CHURCH

When I consider how my brothers and sisters in Christ are suffering

FATHER IN HEAVEN,

I am not rich or pampered, but I have life so easy compared to most people in the world. And when I learn what thousands of my fellow Christians worldwide are encountering and enduring, I am humbled and grieved. Bibles are being confiscated, churches burned, pastors imprisoned and tortured, families torn apart, and many maimed or killed, all because these believers are not ashamed to follow their Lord and Savior, Jesus Christ. I am so weak in my witness, often backing off at the first sign of opposition, and they are so strong, courageous, and faithful. Many rejoice in their persecution and continue to share the gospel. I am one with them, dear Lord. What an example they provide of commitment and discipleship. Strengthen and encourage them, Father. Heal their wounds, protect them, guide them, and release those in prison, I pray. Let them feel your presence and know that their brothers and sisters, though thousands of miles away, are praying for them.

[Paul said,] "I don't know what awaits me, except that the Holy Spirit tells me in city after city that jail and suffering lie ahead. But my life is worth nothing to me unless I use it for finishing the work assigned me by the Lord Jesus—the work of telling others the Good News about the wonderful grace of God." ACTS 20:22-24

DAY 150

A prayer about BEAUTY
When I feel drawn to the world's values

DEAR LORD,

I love all things beautiful because I know that beauty—whether a sparkling waterfall, soaring eagle, canyon panorama, snowcapped mountain range, glorious sunset, innocent baby's smile, toddler's first halting steps and words, stirring symphony, inspiring cathedral, child's painting, or master's work of art—is because of you and from you. If I listen carefully and look closely, I quickly sense that beauty surrounds me and that these glorious sights and sounds can draw me closer to you as I celebrate your perfection. But I also know that the idea of beauty has been co-opted by the world, twisted and presented as a commodity, highlighting youthful, physical looks, sexual appeal, glamour. Airbrushed photos show physically enhanced celebrities posing as role models, the ideal. The whole presentation is so shallow and superficial . . . but enticing. And I confess that often I am drawn to those images and try to measure up. Forgive me, Lord. Help me remember that I am beautiful in your eyes, where it matters, and help me strive for *your* kind of beauty, inside and out.

Charm is deceptive, and beauty does not last; but a [person] who fears the LORD will be greatly praised.
PROVERBS 31:30

A prayer about PURPOSE
When I consider my reason for living

HEAVENLY FATHER,
Sooner or later, everyone asks the big questions in life: Why am I here? What is life all about? What's the purpose for living, for life itself? I probably began thinking seriously about these issues during adolescence, but the questioning intensified in the years that followed as my awareness and perception grew. Also as I matured in my Christian faith, I learned that my purpose should be to glorify you. I am not simply existing in the time allotted between birth and death—my life has meaning. People try to fill the emptiness in their lives with a wide variety of dead-end purposes and counterfeit gods: pleasure, success, money, power, and more. But they're headed in the wrong direction. You spared me from that, Lord, and have given me purpose and joy. I do want to "spread [your] fame throughout the earth." Every day is a meaningful adventure in living for you. Please keep me focused on my purpose, pointing to Christ through my attitude, words, and lifestyle.

I have spared you for a purpose—to show you my power and to spread my fame throughout the earth. EXODUS 9:16

A prayer about EDUCATION
When I know I need to learn

FATHER GOD,
Some days I believe that I am fairly intelligent, that I can read with understanding, that I have specialized knowledge in certain areas and insight into others, and that I can figure out how things work and why certain events happen. But then I am confronted with a profound mystery of life or in Holy Scripture, and I realize how little I know; in fact, I'm just a primary pupil in your school. I don't ever want to stop learning, Lord. I want to be a student of the Word because I want to know more about you, your ways, and your will. Help me to never think that I have arrived spiritually, that I know it all theologically. I don't want to let myself grow complacent in the Christian life. Instead, I want to continue to ask and study and learn. Open my mind and heart to you. Lead me to teachers and mentors who can take me deeper—in person and through their writing and speaking, past and present. More than facts, I want life-changing truths. More than intelligence, I want wisdom. Teach me, omniscient God.

Lead me by your truth and teach me, for you are the God who saves me. All day long I put my hope in you.
PSALM 25:5

DAY 153 *Prayerful Moment*

A prayer about FUTURE DREAMS
When I consider my desires and goals

LORD JESUS,
I have big plans for the future. And I'm prepared to work hard to achieve my goals. But I want to honor you in all I do. I know I should be a good steward of the resources you have entrusted to my care, and I want all my plans to align with your will. I also know I will be tempted to try to get ahead by using means that are not centered on you. Help me resist and make godly choices.

It is pleasant to see dreams come true, but fools refuse to turn from evil to attain them. PROVERBS 13:19

DAY 154 *Prayerful Moment*

A prayer about REBELLIOUSNESS
When I purposely turn away from God

MY HOLY AND MERCIFUL FATHER,
I am painfully aware of how you want me to think and act, but I have disobeyed. I know better and deserve your punishment, but I ask for mercy. I love you, Lord, but I continually fall into the trap of thinking that I know better than you. How foolish I am! Forgive me, Father; please restore our relationship. I submit to your will.

I turned away from God, but then I was sorry. I kicked myself for my stupidity! I was thoroughly ashamed of all I did in my younger days. JEREMIAH 31:19

DAY 155

A prayer about ENVIRONMENT
When I care for my surroundings

DEAR LORD,

Today I was struck by some people's careless disregard for the environment. One street corner I passed, not too far from home, was littered with beer bottles, fast-food wrappers, cans, and scraps of paper. I saw a vacant lot with a discarded Christmas tree, a rusty appliance, a broken bicycle, and other junk. Most parking lots are the final resting place for cigarette butts, candy wrappers, and rubber bands. And a drive through most neighborhoods reveals a number of unkempt yards—weeds and untrimmed hedges threatening to obscure the houses. At Creation you gave the first humans responsibility to care for the earth. I know that I, too, am responsible for your amazing gift of nature. This means that as a good steward, I need to take good care of what you've entrusted to me and use your resources wisely. Thank you for placing me in my "garden." Show me how I can take care of it, and please forgive me when I forget or take it for granted.

God blessed them and said, "Be fruitful and multiply. Fill the earth and govern it. Reign over the fish in the sea, the birds in the sky, and all the animals that scurry along the ground." . . . Then God looked over all he had made, and he saw that it was very good! GENESIS 1:28, 31

A prayer about MAKING A DIFFERENCE IN THE WORLD

When I want to make an impact with my life

LORD OF HEAVEN AND EARTH,
I'm just one person out of billions on earth. Surrounded by powerful forces in government, business, and society, I often feel totally powerless and insignificant. My temptation is to simply fall into a comfortable routine and try my best to be happy. But I know that's not right. I also know that you are all powerful, much greater than any group or institution in the world. Someone has said that God plus one makes a majority, and I want to be that one. You have given me talents, gifts, and abilities to invest wisely for you. I want to use them to truly make a difference, even if that means one person at a time—nothing grand—just you and me working together to change lives. You said that someone with faith as small as a mustard seed could move mountains. I want to change the world, beginning here, with me.

"You don't have enough faith," Jesus told [the disciples]. "I tell you the truth, if you had faith even as small as a mustard seed, you could say to this mountain, 'Move from here to there,' and it would move. Nothing would be impossible." MATTHEW 17:20

DAY 157

A prayer about GOALS
When I strive to reach my objectives

SOVEREIGN LORD,
As a goal-oriented person, I have objectives and specific outcomes in sight, and I work hard to accomplish them. I take this approach in all areas—career, finances, friendships, and even my spiritual life. This approach has served me well because I get things done. I love checking items off the to-do list. But I have become increasingly aware of weaknesses in this approach. Sometimes I use less than the best means to reach an end. Then I rationalize by pointing to the eventual good result. But I know that *everything* I do should please you—ends and means. Forgive me. I also sense that this goal-orientation keeps me looking toward the future, sometimes at the expense and neglect of the present. So I hurry ahead and miss important people and events right *now*. Thank you for *all* your gifts, especially my family and friends. Please help me relax as I "waste" time with them. And, of course, I want my goals to be in line with your will, so I pray for your guidance in setting them.

Whether we are here in this body or away from this body, our goal is to please him. 2 CORINTHIANS 5:9

DAY 158

A prayer about THOUGHTS
When my mind needs changing

HEAVENLY FATHER,
My thought life needs help. Usually that's where specific sins begin, from thoughts of lust, jealousy, self-righteousness, anger, or revenge. My focus can translate into actions of the wrong kind. At times negative thoughts just pop into my mind, but often they are stimulated by what I see, hear, read, or feel. Because I am a sinner, my first instinct is to go where my mind takes me—to what is false, dishonorable, wrong, impure, unlovely, and despicable. My thoughts need to be fixed elsewhere, on whatever is "excellent and worthy of praise," on what glorifies you. Change my mind, Father; purify my way of thinking. When media draw my attention and thoughts to sinful activities, give me strength to change channels or turn off the TV, shut down the web page, toss the magazine, choose another book, or turn to a Christian radio station. In my social interactions, focus my attention on people's strengths, seeing the good in them. Change me from a critical faultfinder to a praise giver. And in every situation, please help me think of you.

Fix your thoughts on what is true, and honorable, and right, and pure, and lovely, and admirable. Think about things that are excellent and worthy of praise. PHILIPPIANS 4:8

DAY 159

A prayer about FOCUS
When I take my eyes off Christ

SAVIOR,
I know that one of the most important keys to running well and finishing strong is to stay focused on the goal. Runners who begin to think about every ache and pain get discouraged and consider quitting the race. Those who are distracted by intriguing sights and sounds on either side of the course can begin to slow, meander, or fall, as they lose sight of the way. I am like both kinds of runners at times. I can let physical and emotional pain slow my pace. Or I can allow temptations and worldly concerns pull me off course. This world presents distractions and enticements at every turn. Mine include others' opinions of me, personal security, physical appearance and health, notable achievements, and more. I need to keep focused on you and your will, Jesus. I need your spiritual blinders to keep me from being drawn off course. You, your glory, your prize are all I desire. Please help me to always look forward, keeping my eyes on you.

Obviously, I'm not trying to win the approval of people, but of God. If pleasing people were my goal, I would not be Christ's servant. GALATIANS 1:10

DAY 160 *Prayerful Moment*

A prayer about NEW CREATION
When I know I am being transformed

FATHER,
Born in sin, I live in a fallen world, and life would be hopeless except for your promise to make all things new. You began that process in me when I first trusted Christ as my Savior; you made me into a "new creation" and are transforming me. I can't wait to see what you will do next in me and through me. Thank you, blessed Creator.

It doesn't matter whether we have been circumcised or not. What counts is whether we have been transformed into a new creation. GALATIANS 6:15

DAY 161 *Prayerful Moment*

A prayer about NEIGHBORS
When I consider the people who live near me

SAVIOR,
I have many "neighbors"; you say that I am to love them all. This is difficult to do. Often they annoy me by failing to care for their property, parking their cars in front of my house, or making noise late into the night. Please help me see them as people you love and for whom you died. Then show me how I can love my neighbor too.

A second [commandment] is equally important: "Love your neighbor as yourself." The entire law and all the demands of the prophets are based on these two commandments. MATTHEW 22:39-40

A prayer about RELATIONSHIPS
When I consider the people in my life

GRACIOUS HEAVENLY FATHER,

I am a social being because you created me that way. Adam had a perfect environment, but you proclaimed, "It is not good for the man to be alone"—and you gave him Eve. We need to love and be loved. Thank you, God, for all the people you have brought into my life. First, thank you for family—they have watched my growth and have nurtured, disciplined, served, and cheered me. Then, thank you for the gift of friends who accept, correct, and encourage me. Both groups love me, even though they know the real me, my weaknesses, mistakes, and all. And thank you for my Christian family, brothers and sisters who teach me, serve shoulder to shoulder with me, and hold me accountable to your Word. I have relationships with many others: coworkers, neighbors, teachers, merchants, and more. What amazing gifts—I am not alone! And I know you are using them to shape me into your kind of person. I want to be a great family member, friend, fellow believer, neighbor, and citizen. Help me.

The LORD God said, "It is not good for the man to be alone. I will make a helper who is just right for him."
GENESIS 2:18

DAY 163

A prayer about SATAN
When I feel under attack

HEAVENLY FATHER,
I know I can become complacent in my faith, even though you have warned me about the enemy. Despite popular representations, he is real and dangerous, a devouring "lion" often disguised as something good. You have called Satan a liar and the Accuser, and he uses both tactics in bombarding me, lying about you and reminding me of my failures and sins. I have felt under heavy attack, with the devil's accusations swirling about in my mind and obstacles being placed in my way. So I ask you to bind Satan, Father. Close my ears to his lies and open them to your truth. You have said I should resist the devil, and I do. Right now, through your power, I reject his words and influence. I know, Lord, that this doesn't end the struggle because the enemy is always near, using doubts, temptations, and excuses to keep me from following you closely. So I ask for awareness of his wiles and for strength to counteract them. You are all powerful, Lord. The devil is no match.

Stay alert! Watch out for your great enemy, the devil. He prowls around like a roaring lion, looking for someone to devour. 1 PETER 5:8

DAY 164

A prayer about ROLE MODELS
When I think about who is influencing me

LORD ABOVE,

Throughout my life people have influenced me greatly by how they lived and what they taught. Early on, parents and teachers made the most powerful impact. Then came coaches, directors, pastors, and youth leaders. Along the way I was impressed by close friends. I can see that I picked up my values by emulating them. This was not a conscious process, but I changed through their influence. Some of my choices of role models were not the best, but thank you for giving me godly men and women who pointed me to you. That's in the past, but I know I am still influenced by others whom I admire. I still need someone to coach me. So I pray for new role models who will encourage and prod me to live for you. And please avert my gaze from those who would lead me the wrong way. My primary example should be Jesus—I need to keep watching him. I also want to *be* a godly example for those who look up to me, modeling your values.

Remember your leaders who taught you the word of God. Think of all the good that has come from their lives, and follow the example of their faith. HEBREWS 13:7

DAY 165

A prayer about GOD'S WILL
When I need guidance

LORD,

I want what you want, to do your will. My usual way of operating is to gather as much relevant information as I can. Then, based on that information, I make an informed decision about the way to go and I move ahead. It's a deliberate process. I am not an impulsive person and not driven by emotions. So I usually try to do what is reasonable and right. The problem, however, is that I tend to be self-reliant and so self-confident that I do everything on my own, with no thought of you. How foolish! Forgive me, Lord. I need you at every turn, every step of the way, in every decision. You alone know the best way for me, the path to take. But why do I turn to you only when I'm confused or in trouble? I need you in the rain and darkness, yes, but also in the sunlight. You reveal your will through your Word, prayer, and others. I trust you, Lord. Please guide me, I pray, as I determine to live your way every day.

Trust in the LORD with all your heart; do not depend on your own understanding. Seek his will in all you do, and he will show you which path to take. PROVERBS 3:5-6

DAY 166

A prayer about WASTE

When I squander opportunities and resources

DEAR LORD,

As a responsible manager of the precious resources you have entrusted to me, I don't want to be guilty of misusing or wasting time, such as following every e-mail trail and Internet link or subjecting myself to vacuous, immoral entertainment or godless ideas. I also need to carefully invest my personal gifts, financial resources, relationships, and opportunities for your glory. But according to your Word, "waste" has a place if I am lavishing my attention and resources on you. When a woman anointed Jesus with expensive perfume at the dinner table in Bethany, his disciples saw it as a waste, but he commended her for her act of worship. The woman understood who you were and knew exactly what she was doing. I'm afraid that I see myself in those men, focused on the apparent waste and missing the point. I love you, Lord, and want to honor you in all I do. Please show me how and when to spend extravagantly in my worship and devotion to you.

The disciples were indignant. . . . "What a waste!" they said.
MATTHEW 26:8

DAY 167 *Prayerful Moment*

A prayer about PERSEVERANCE
When I consider my life of faith

PRECIOUS SAVIOR,
You endured the Cross—nothing I face compares to your physical pain and the agony of bearing all our sin. Yet I often let minor setbacks push me off course or I allow sins to trip me. I want to run this life race *for* you and *with* you. Please give me strength and resolve to run well and finish strong.

Let us strip off every weight that slows us down, especially the sin that so easily trips us up. And let us run with endurance the race God has set before us.
HEBREWS 12:1

DAY 168 *Prayerful Moment*

A prayer about SPIRITUAL THIRST
When I need to drink from God's springs

JESUS,
People can't live without water very long; the same is true with spiritual thirst. You told the Samaritan woman about living water, and I drank from that spring when I trusted you as my Savior. But lately I've been dry, and I need to be refreshed, renewed. Lead me again to your waters. I need you, Jesus. Quench my thirsty soul.

Those who drink the water I give will never be thirsty again. It becomes a fresh, bubbling spring within them, giving them eternal life. JOHN 4:14

DAY 169

A prayer about CHURCH

When I gather with my brothers and sisters in Christ

DEAR SAVIOR,

You told Peter and the other disciples that you would build your church, the assembled gathering of those who have trusted you as Savior, and that all of hell's powers will not be able to stop it. I love your church—universal and local. As a collection of human beings, we are fallible and sinful, yet you have called us together and given us the challenge and opportunity to represent you on earth and to spread your word. Since we are your body, the world should see you in us, and I pray that they do. Thank you for my brothers and sisters in the faith; we are one, regardless of the specific churches we attend. And thank you for my local body of believers, where we can worship, learn, and serve together and challenge and encourage one another. Through the years my fellow believers have provided so much comfort and direction for me. Please strengthen and empower our pastor and other church leaders. Empower me to make your church your home, being true to the Word and glorifying you in all we do.

God has put all things under the authority of Christ and has made him head over all things for the benefit of the church. And the church is his body; it is made full and complete by Christ, who fills all things everywhere with himself.

EPHESIANS 1:22-23

DAY 170

A prayer about FAMILY
When I think about those who love me

DEAR HEAVENLY FATHER,

What a gift you have given me—family. At every stage of my life, they have been with me, whether close or extended; they make me who I am. Certainly they are not perfect; and knowing each other so well, we can easily spot each other's flaws. But we belong to each other. I confess that often I look past them, assuming that they will always be there, and obsess instead about what I don't have. Yet my own flesh and blood and many others surround and care for me. Even when I am separated by distance or death from my physical family, I have close friends nearby with whom I can share my deepest feelings, thoughts, fears, and dreams. What a blessing! Significant in this family are those with whom I share spiritual DNA, my brothers and sisters in Christ. And to think that this family of God extends beyond my small circle in this neighborhood to every community across the nation and around the world—from millennia past and into the future. Thank you, Lord!

God decided in advance to adopt us into his own family by bringing us to himself through Jesus Christ. This is what he wanted to do, and it gave him great pleasure.

EPHESIANS 1:5

DAY 171

A prayer about PROGRESS
When I look back and then ahead

HOLY SPIRIT,
Looking at pictures of myself from even just a year or two ago, I can't believe how much I've changed physically. I couldn't see the changes as they were occurring, only now as I look back. I know I have grown spiritually, too, Spirit of God—in the moments, days, weeks, months, and years of your working in me. I certainly am not where I need to be, but I am making progress. I also know I'm not where I will be, because of your transforming power. Your promise to make me more and more like Christ gives me hope, especially when my sins and mistakes seem to stop my progress or move me backward and when I encounter challenges and conflicts. At times I wonder if I've grown at all when I blunder and act so spiritually immature or fall back into a destructive pattern. But I *know* you are in me, doing your work. Please forgive me for not listening to your promptings, heeding your warnings, or following your guidance. I want to continue to progress with you.

The Lord—who is the Spirit—makes us more and more like him as we are changed into his glorious image.
2 CORINTHIANS 3:18

A prayer about THE INCARNATION
When I think of what Jesus did for me

MY SAVIOR, MY GOD,
You became a human person, a baby. The word *incarnation* says it all, but that sounds technical and theological. It just means something like, "with meat on"; in other words, you "put on flesh," human flesh, a body. The spirit "became flesh," one of us—someone just like me. Every year at Christmas, we celebrate your birth with simple plays, grand pageants, and cantatas, featuring the little baby in the manger surrounded by Mary and Joseph, animals and shepherds. Then kings come bearing gifts. The story is familiar, but we can miss the miracle. The Eternal became mortal. The All-powerful became weak. The Sovereign became servant. The Everything became nothing. The Holy One became sin. I worship and adore you, Jesus. I know you came, lived, died, and rose for all who believe, but you also came for *me*. Not only did you submit yourself to all the limitations of being a man, but you submitted yourself to death, to the Cross. Words fail me as I try to express how I feel. I love you, Savior.

Though he was God, he did not think of equality with God as something to cling to. Instead, he gave up his divine privileges; he took the humble position of a slave and was born as a human being. When he appeared in human form, he humbled himself in obedience to God and died a criminal's death on a cross. PHILIPPIANS 2:6-8

DAY 173

A prayer about LONELINESS
When I feel all alone

DEAR LORD,

The feeling does not hit often, but loneliness can descend like a heavy mist, obscuring my vision and clouding my mind and emotions. At times it happens when a loved one leaves, and I sense the absence often over the next few days. That's to be expected, I suppose. But the feeling also comes at night or even suddenly during the day. That happened today. I need you always, Lord, but especially in these moments when I seem isolated and feel abandoned and alone. Please be close, Lord. Make your presence palpable. I know that many of my brothers and sisters in Christ are in prisons, often having been torn from their loved ones. Totally isolated, they rejoice in their relationship with you, grateful for the opportunity to suffer for you and affirming that you are with them at every moment. I pray that I may have their kind of courage, faith, and sensitivity to you. Help me trust you, knowing (to paraphrase Corrie ten Boom) that no matter how deep the pit, you are deeper still.

Those who know your name trust in you, for you, O LORD, do not abandon those who search for you. PSALM 9:10

DAY 174 *Prayerful Moment*

A prayer about RESTITUTION
When I need to make things right

GOD,

I accidentally broke a friend's prized possession. This friend forgave me and said not to worry about it, but I know I should obey you, even though it won't be cheap. Help me make full restitution. I want to live your way.

You must give back whatever you stole, or the money you took by extortion, or the security deposit, or the lost property you found, or anything obtained by swearing falsely. You must make restitution by paying the full price plus an additional 20 percent to the person you have harmed.
LEVITICUS 6:4-5

DAY 175 *Prayerful Moment*

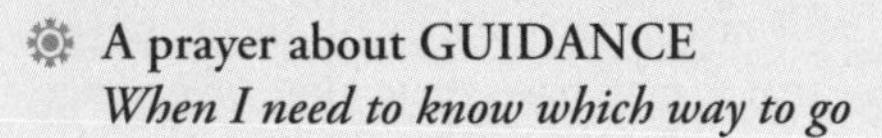

A prayer about GUIDANCE
When I need to know which way to go

DEAR LORD,

There is a choice I have to make. I've talked with you about this often. I've also researched the issue and sought advice from those whose counsel I trust. Then I prayed again. All the options are good—none violate your Word. So I expect you to work through my mind as I make the final decision. Guide me, Lord. I want to do your will.

Lead me in the right path, O LORD, or my enemies will conquer me. Make your way plain for me to follow.
PSALM 5:8

A prayer about MORALITY
When I encounter relativism

SOVEREIGN GOD,

The question of personal behavior is getting fuzzy these days without a sense of right and wrong. Intellectual elites assert that no absolutes exist, morality depends on the person, and in this age of political correctness, no one should push his or her moral standards on anyone else. So most seem to think that we should be able to do whatever feels good as long as no one gets hurt. I know that way of thinking is completely false. We definitely have rights and wrongs, because you have revealed your will and absolute truth in your Word, the Bible. I get so frustrated and tired, Lord, fighting the anti-God, relativistic attitudes and immorality. Your moral law is clearly stated in the Ten Commandments, but people turn their backs on you. My heart breaks to see so many people give in and go that way. Give me strength to persevere and continue to resist the immoral temptations pushing in on all sides. And help me to lovingly and patiently point my friends to you and your truth.

There will be false teachers among you. They will cleverly teach destructive heresies and even deny the Master who bought them. In this way, they will bring sudden destruction on themselves. Many will follow their evil teaching and shameful immorality. And because of these teachers, the way of truth will be slandered. 2 PETER 2:1-2

A prayer about HARD WORK
When I try to earn God's favor

GRACIOUS GOD,
I have worked hard all my life. Nothing has ever come easy, and I have given everything my best effort. Sometimes the results were quite positive; other times, not so much. But I always felt good about giving my all. I brought that same work ethic and self-reliance to the Christian life and threw myself into every type of spiritual task imaginable: reading the Bible, praying, serving, raising money, teaching, singing, and generally being at church for every event possible. Until I burned out in all my religious effort. I realize now that you don't rate me on the amount of work I do for you and that I was trying to earn your favor. Instead, I need to trust you and allow you to do your work in me and through me. I know you don't want me to be lazy, but I should work hard for your Kingdom as a *result* of being saved, not *in order* to be saved. Thank you that all the work of salvation was done on the cross through Christ.

God saved you by his grace when you believed. And you can't take credit for this; it is a gift from God. Salvation is not a reward for the good things we have done, so none of us can boast about it. EPHESIANS 2:8-9

DAY 178

A prayer about MAKING A GOOD IMPRESSION

When I am concerned about what others think of me

PRECIOUS SAVIOR,

I admit that I often think about others' opinions of me personally and what they think of how I look and act. That can be a trap if my focus is on myself. And I can be a phony if my image doesn't match the real me. But my deepest desire, Jesus, is to make a good impression for you. I want people to see joy, purpose, and hope. My prayer is that people who don't know I am a Christian will wonder about what makes the difference in my life. And I want those who *do* know that I follow you to see you in me. My life should radiate a good impression of you and the new life you give. When the crowd is going the wrong way, please give me the courage to stay true, turn, and go your way. In potentially ethics-compromising situations, give me strength to do what is right. During times of crisis and stress, give me faith to rely on you. May people be drawn to you through my life.

This is how the LORD responds: "If you return to me, I will restore you so you can continue to serve me. If you speak good words rather than worthless ones, you will be my spokesman. You must influence them; do not let them influence you!"
JEREMIAH 15:19

A prayer about GOD'S CALL
When I think about effectively serving the Savior

O LORD,
I admit that I get a bit uneasy when I hear someone say, "God called me . . ." to a specific task or ministry. And I feel very uncomfortable when a church leader asserts that God's people should not be involved in various ministries (teaching Sunday school, singing in the choir, visiting people in the hospital, serving as a church officer, and so forth) unless they have been called. What does that mean, Lord? I haven't heard your voice, received a notice in the mail, or seen writing in the sky. I have your Word, and as I read and study, I see that "call" is mentioned several times. I know that you have chosen and called me to come to you. You have also appointed me to do your work in the world, using my spiritual gifts to build up the church and share the good news with others. So please help me know where I can best serve you, living out your will for me. I want to be faithful, responding to your clear call.

Having chosen them, he called them to come to him. And having called them, he gave them right standing with himself. And having given them right standing, he gave them his glory. ROMANS 8:30

DAY 180

A prayer about RESCUE
When I am in deep trouble

ALMIGHTY GOD,

I am mired in the quicksand of trouble and sinking fast. It feels as though everything is closing in, and try as I might, I can't get out. Help me, I pray. I am desperate! You are all powerful, Lord, and can do anything. So please provide me *your* way out of this dilemma. Show me what to do and give me the strength to follow through. In the Old Testament I read about Shadrach, Meshach, and Abednego who, as they were about to be burned alive, confidently told Nebuchadnezzar that you would rescue them. But that if you did not, they would die faithfully serving and worshiping you alone. Oh, may that be my attitude, Lord. I know you *can* rescue me, but if you choose not to, please help me accept your decision. More than anything, I want your will to be done and for my life to honor and glorify you.

If we are thrown into the blazing furnace, the God whom we serve is able to save us. He will rescue us from your power, Your Majesty. But even if he doesn't, we want to make it clear to you, Your Majesty, that we will never serve your gods or worship the gold statue you have set up.
DANIEL 3:17-18

DAY 181 *Prayerful Moment*

A prayer about SUCCESS
When I push to achieve

JESUS,
Solomon saw that "most people are motivated to success" but proclaimed it a meaningless pursuit. Lord, you told your disciples, who were eager to gain recognition and power, that the first would be last and that gaining the world is a waste of time. Shocking. Countercultural. But nothing compares to knowing you, Savior. Help me choose what is most important—being successful in pursuing you.

I observed that most people are motivated to success because they envy their neighbors. But this, too, is meaningless—like chasing the wind. ECCLESIASTES 4:4

DAY 182 *Prayerful Moment*

A prayer about PRIORITIES
When I analyze what I am doing

SOVEREIGN LORD,
I often find myself racing from one crisis, deadline, or e-mail to the next. In the process I can neglect what I should be paying attention to. I realize this may mean I need to get better organized, but it also may reveal a faulty mind-set. Help me, I pray, to reorganize my mind around your priorities and values.

What do you benefit if you gain the whole world but lose your own soul? Is anything worth more than your soul?
MATTHEW 16:26

DAY 183

A prayer about GOD'S PRESENCE
When I sense my Lord is near

SPIRIT OF GOD,
Some speak of feeling close to you in special settings: while listening to a musical masterpiece, singing an emotive worship song, hearing a stirring personal testimony, responding to a powerful sermon, or exulting in your magnificent creation. Certainly you are in those places. But I sensed your presence today, all day, in many other ways. In the morning, as I moved to my first responsibilities, phrases from your Word kept coming to mind. Sometimes they were from the passage I had read earlier; at other times, from verses I had memorized. Later, I saw evidence of you in direct answers to my prayers. I also know you were, and are, working behind the scenes, weaving together all things for my good and your glory. You are with me in my quiet moments and in the noise and clutter of everyday life. We stand together in my victories and defeats, highs and lows, joys and sorrows. You are also with me in every place—home, neighborhood, work, church, gym, restaurant, theater, airplane. Thank you, Lord.

I can never escape from your Spirit! I can never get away from your presence! PSALM 139:7

A prayer about HABITS

When I need to break bad practices

SPIRIT OF GOD,

A friend implied that I had developed some bad habits, harmful to me and to my relationship with you. My first response was denial. Then I made excuses, rationalizing my behavior as normal and expected, especially for someone in my situation. But I was just trying to convince myself; I certainly fooled no one else. Seeing another person's problem is easy—it's obvious. However, I was blind to my own issues and shortcomings. I know that the start is simply realizing where I am, and I do. I have a problem, Lord, and I need your help. Just determining and trying to be different may work for a short time but won't accomplish much long term. I need to break my old and current routines and establish new, positive habits that bring me closer to you. Please, Holy Spirit, continue to change my desires, and help me see what new steps I should take. Then, give me the commitment and courage to take them. And, I pray, please keep bringing friends alongside me who will encourage me and hold me accountable.

Do not let sin control the way you live; do not give in to sinful desires. Do not let any part of your body become an instrument of evil to serve sin. Instead, give yourselves completely to God, for you were dead, but now you have new life. So use your whole body as an instrument to do what is right for the glory of God. ROMANS 6:12-13

DAY 185

A prayer about THE SABBATH
When I need the day of rest

LOVING CREATOR,

You created the heavens and the earth in six days and set aside the next day for rest. Then you commanded your people to dedicate every seventh day—the Sabbath—to worship and rest. I need regular Sabbath days, Lord, because I am tired and because you created human beings with that necessary life rhythm. I forget that and work hard to fill just about every waking moment of the week with activity. Even worship and other church events and responsibilities have succumbed as I frenetically run from one activity to another. Maybe I have a messiah complex, or perhaps I don't want to stop and listen to you, afraid of what I might hear. But living this way is unhealthy and wrong. Beyond needing a break from my obsessive agenda, I need concentrated time with you, quality time. Please show me what to unload or leave behind, how to rearrange my schedule. The ancient Sabbath began at sundown, so help me prepare the night before, giving me a full seventh day to spend with you.

Remember to observe the Sabbath day by keeping it holy.
EXODUS 20:8

DAY 186

A prayer about COWORKERS
When I think about my colleagues

DEAR LORD,
I spend so much time each week with select groups as we work to reach our goals together. With one set I earn a living, investing eight hours daily during the week. With another, friends at church and in other ministries, I minister in the evenings and on weekends. These coworkers know—almost as well as my family does—my strengths and weaknesses, work habits, response to supervision, commitment to the mission, interests, values, and reactions under pressure. And I know them—their struggles, hurts, loves, desires, challenges, and dreams. These people certainly know I'm not perfect, because they have seen my miscues up close and personal. And they can see through any facade or image I may attempt to project; for example, when I pretend to be something I'm not. In other words, they know the real me. My hope—my prayer—is that the real me is what you want me to be. I want them to see Christ in everything I do . . . in my focus, choices, reactions, stewardship, conversations, values, and relationships.

Whatever you do or say, do it as a representative of the Lord Jesus, giving thanks through him to God the Father.
COLOSSIANS 3:17

DAY 187

A prayer about THE BODY OF CHRIST
When I consider the worldwide family of God

SAVIOR,

When I first put my trust in you, I became a member of your family, your "body." Every week I gather with this family for instruction, fellowship, and worship. We serve, encourage, and challenge one another. But your body goes beyond my local church to include brothers and sisters of all ages, worldwide, through the centuries. By your grace, these boys, girls, men, and women live in every corner and culture of the earth, with every language and every station in life. They come in the whole human spectrum—as the Sunday school song proclaims, "Red and yellow, black and white, all are precious in [your] sight!" Whatever the differences, all believers are one in you. I know that so many of my brothers and sisters are suffering—mocked, beaten, ostracized, imprisoned, tortured, and even martyred for their faith. In their lands, following you is outlawed. Their only crime is professing your name. Be with them, Lord. By your Spirit strengthen and encourage them. And dear Savior, give me the courage to stand with them for you, regardless of the cost.

Some of us are Jews, some are Gentiles, some are slaves, and some are free. But we have all been baptized into one body by one Spirit, and we all share the same Spirit.

1 CORINTHIANS 12:13

DAY 188 *Prayerful Moment*

A prayer about DESIRES
When I wonder about what I want

GOD ABOVE,
I get confused at times about what I want in life. With so many options, I feel pulled this way and that. I confess that I often find myself desiring something that does not honor you. But I delight in *you*, Lord—I want to match my desires with yours, to be your person, fully.

Remember and obey all the commands of the LORD instead of following your own desires. NUMBERS 15:39

DAY 189 *Prayerful Moment*

A prayer about AMEN
When I know that my prayers are heard

FATHER,
Often my prayers become routine, ending abruptly with, "In Jesus' name, amen." Forgive me for rushing those words. I am nothing without Jesus, and I can come to you only because of him. "Amen" has become trite, but it means "Yes!"—an exclamation point at the end of my prayer-sentence. I affirm that I believe what I am saying, that I believe in you. I know you hear me and will answer me. Amen!

All of God's promises have been fulfilled in Christ with a resounding "Yes!" And through Christ, our "Amen" . . . ascends to God for his glory. 2 CORINTHIANS 1:20

DAY 190

A prayer about TIME
When I make plans

DEAR LORD,

When I was a child, a year seemed a long time because it comprised a significant percentage of my life to that point. I could hardly imagine living to thirty—so many years away. As I grew older, I thought about my future—education, career, marriage, and other dreams—confident that I would fulfill them; it was just a matter of time. Now looking back, I wonder how those years slipped by so quickly. I still make plans, Lord, but I have learned to hold them loosely because I am *not* you and do not know what will happen. You have also taught me that I should make the most of today because tomorrow is not promised. This means I should not wait for a better time to use my gifts, to comfort the hurting, to share the gospel, and to invest my resources for your Kingdom. Life truly is short, Lord. Thank you for the years you have given me and for all the blessings they contained. I will continue to plan, but I know that your plans will prevail.

Look here, you who say, "Today or tomorrow we are going to a certain town and will stay there a year. We will do business there and make a profit." How do you know what your life will be like tomorrow? Your life is like the morning fog—it's here a little while, then it's gone. What you ought to say is, "If the Lord wants us to, we will live and do this or that."

JAMES 4:13-15

DAY 191

A prayer about HONESTY
When I am tempted to lie or steal

HEAVENLY FATHER,

I know you want me to display the highest integrity in everything I do—in my conversations, with the government, in the workplace, when I'm shopping—to be truthful and honest in *all* my dealings. But sometimes I am tempted to cut corners a bit. When I receive too much change at a restaurant, for example, I can easily rationalize that I deserve it; after all, it's the waitstaff's mistake, and this makes up for when I was overcharged, and so forth. Or when I am confronted about something I have done, my first thought is to deny the truth, blame someone else, or make excuses. And income tax preparation is a definite pressure point for being honest. I know that you see everything and know my thoughts and that you forgive me of my sins even before I do them. But your Word makes very clear that you expect your people to be honest. I want to be totally open with you, Lord. And I want my *first* inclination to be to do what is right.

LORD, you are searching for honesty. JEREMIAH 5:3

DAY 192

A prayer about MAKING ENDS MEET
When my bills keep mounting

AWESOME GOD,
I know that you "own the cattle on a thousand hills," that everything belongs to you. In comparison, the wealthiest person on earth has absolutely nothing. I certainly am far from financially secure, and right now, as I look at the mounting stack of bills, I'm feeling a bit desperate. In fact, I can't see any way out of this mess. You have trusted me with resources; though they are meager by many standards, you still expect me to be a good steward and use them wisely. So please give me wisdom, Lord, for how I can cut expenses, increase income, and invest for the Kingdom. And please increase my faith. Right now things don't *look* promising, but you said that your followers should live by believing and not by seeing. So I need to know that what I am going through now is a faith-stretching experience. And if this is what I need, keep stretching me; I *do* want to live by faith. So right now I pray for provision, guidance, and faith.

All the animals of the forest are mine, and I own the cattle on a thousand hills. PSALM 50:10

DAY 193

A prayer about ADOPTION

When I know that I am God's child, chosen by him

MY FATHER,

I am so thankful that I can call you Father—*Dad.* I have an earthly family whom I love very much. I am like my earthly parents, either through genetics or environment (or both). Then, when I put my trust in Christ, you changed me and made me a member of your family. I was born again. But the Bible also says that I am adopted. This means you *chose* me and brought me home. No matter where I am, what I feel, or what I am going through, I know I belong to you, that you are with me and are looking out for me. I also know that I am becoming more and more like you. Because I am your beloved child, when I feel afraid or lost, you will find me; when I am joyful, you celebrate with me; as I run life's race, you cheer me on as my biggest fan! And when I hurt, you comfort me, drawing me close in your loving arms. At those times—and now—I cry, "Hold me, Daddy."

You have not received a spirit that makes you fearful slaves. Instead, you received God's Spirit when he adopted you as his own children. Now we call him, "Abba, Father."
ROMANS 8:15

DAY 194

A prayer about GIVING

When I see a need to be met

DEAR GOD,

You know I like to *receive* gifts—birthdays, Christmas, whatever the occasion. At first I didn't like it when I seemed to be giving out more than I was getting, but over the years, I have been learning about stewardship and my responsibility to help others. You said, "It is more blessed to give than to receive"—counterintuitive but so true. Whether I put cash in the offering plate at church, write a check for a ministry or missionary, donate to a local charity, or take meals to a needy family, I have been learning the joy of giving, even sacrificially. Please help me to loosen my grasp on my money, possessions, and time. I want to be the kind of person who gives generously to meet needs that you bring my way, not out of obligation or duty but because I really *want to*. So do your work on my heart, changing my desires. In reality, all I have belongs to you, so I want to invest those resources for your Kingdom. Please don't let my possessions possess me.

You must each decide in your heart how much to give. And don't give reluctantly or in response to pressure. "For God loves a person who gives cheerfully." 2 CORINTHIANS 9:7

DAY 195 *Prayerful Moment*

A prayer about ARGUING
When I'm having a disagreement

LORD,

I don't enjoy confrontation and would like to get along with everyone. But I know that won't always happen. Today I disagreed with a friend, the argument escalated, and we parted upset. Help me, Father, to know when to stand my ground and when to back off. And in this case, to stay true to what I believe and yet keep my friendship. Give me the words to say when I talk with my friend tomorrow. I want to honor you in all I do.

Arguments separate friends like a gate locked with bars.
PROVERBS 18:19

DAY 196 *Prayerful Moment*

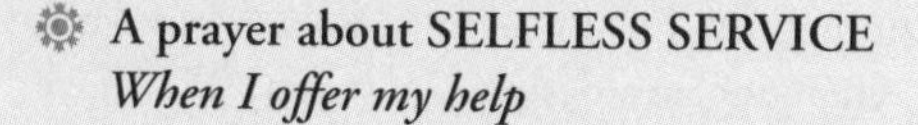

A prayer about SELFLESS SERVICE
When I offer my help

LORD,

Occasionally I have given up a free evening or weekend to help with a service opportunity and have enjoyed the experience. But I wonder if I serve out of pride or guilt. Serving didn't cost much, and I wonder if I would have volunteered if it had. Change my heart, God. Help me love people and give *selflessly*, with no prospects of gaining anything in return.

All of you, serve each other in humility, for "God opposes the proud but favors the humble." 1 PETER 5:5

DAY 197

A prayer about SPIRITUAL GIFTS
When I want God to use me

ALMIGHTY GOD,
I'm confused. In the New Testament, especially the Epistles, I read about special gifts given to each believer by the Holy Spirit, but I don't feel gifted. I want to serve you in the church and in the world, but compared to others, I don't seem to have much to offer. So I ask for insight into my personal mix of spiritual gifts. At one point, I thought I was gifted in a certain way, but my attempts at exercising it were disastrous. So I backed off, fearful of taking another risk. But I would like to help "equip God's people to do his work and build up the church." You have shown me that I am unique, special, so I shouldn't expect to be like anyone else. And I have learned that every member of the body of Christ is significant and plays an important role, not just the leaders, teachers, and pastors. So please help me not to be envious of someone else's gifts. Show me, lead me, and empower me, I pray.

These are the gifts Christ gave to the church: the apostles, the prophets, the evangelists, and the pastors and teachers. Their responsibility is to equip God's people to do his work and build up the church, the body of Christ. This will continue until we all come to such unity in our faith and knowledge of God's Son that we will be mature in the Lord, measuring up to the full and complete standard of Christ.
EPHESIANS 4:11-13

DAY 198

A prayer about SELF-ESTEEM
When I feel worthless

MY FATHER IN HEAVEN,

I have messed up often this week with substandard performance, relationship issues, and sin. I know you have forgiven me, but right now I am feeling nearly worthless, especially when I compare myself to others. Many accomplish more, look better, and seem more spiritual. Thank you for reminding me of Jesus' words to his disciples about your loving concern for every sparrow. I, too, need to remember that you value me much more than a whole flock of sparrows! And I know that through Paul you say I am your "masterpiece." Right now I don't feel much like a fine work of art or marvelous in any way. So please show me how I can use my God-given abilities and gifts to do good things for you. I want you to use me, but right now I'm unsure how that will work out. Thankfully your work in the world does not depend on me and my efforts but on you and your mighty power. I am grateful for the privilege of serving you any way I can.

We are God's masterpiece. He has created us anew in Christ Jesus, so we can do the good things he planned for us long ago.
EPHESIANS 2:10

DAY 199

A prayer about QUESTIONS
When I wonder

MAKER OF HEAVEN AND EARTH,
You created everything, and the entirety belongs to you. My all-powerful God, you also are all knowing; nothing is too difficult for you. You know I have questions; but you also know the answers before I even ask. You are the awesome Lord, but you also are my Father, and you invite me to come into your presence with all my issues, including my doubts, fears, and queries. In Scripture I read how many of your choicest servants spoke harsh words to you, even questioning your actions—Job, David, Jeremiah, Habakkuk—so I know I can talk with you about anything. I have many questions: Why do you allow such tragedy and suffering in the world, especially to children? Why do evil people seem to get away with their terrible deeds? Why did my loved one die? What will happen in the Middle East? What will become of me? Certainly answers would be nice, but I know you are good and are working your purposes in the world and in my life. More than answers, I want you.

LORD, you always give me justice when I bring a case before you. So let me bring you this complaint: Why are the wicked so prosperous? Why are evil people so happy?
JEREMIAH 12:1

DAY 200

A prayer about LOVE FOR BELIEVERS
When I deal with other followers of Christ

LORD JESUS,

When I trusted you as Savior, I became part of your family, with millions of brothers and sisters worldwide. Your family spans millennia and includes men, women, boys, and girls of every race, nation, and culture. Even with our differences, we are unified through faith and by you. Yet at times I clash with believers close to home. Although we share nationality and characteristics, we conflict and clash in other areas. I know I am supposed to *love* them, all of them, but some bother me because of theology. With others the problem is their worship style. To be honest, I have the toughest time with people in my own congregation. At times I find a personality trait quite irritating. Often we have differences of opinion (and how to express them). And sometimes the issue is lifestyle choices. You told the disciples that the world should know we follow you by our love for each other. I pray for that ability. Change me, helping me to choose to serve them and making us truly one.

I am giving you a new commandment: Love each other. Just as I have loved you, you should love each other. Your love for one another will prove to the world that you are my disciples.
JOHN 13:34-35

DAY 201

A prayer about DIRECTION

When I wonder which path to take

DEAR LORD,

Over the years I have been in many discussions about how to know God's will. And I've counseled others about that issue. So until recent events, I thought I had it covered. That is, I had a reasonable answer that seemed biblical. But now I have come to a fork in the road, a decision point, and I'm not sure which way to turn. The situation is one where I don't have to choose between good and bad, because both paths seem good. So what should I do? Those who need to know my choice are pressing for an answer, Father. Thank you for giving me these options. But now I need direction. I want to follow your lead in all that I do, to honor you with my choices and attitudes, my words and deeds. I've prayed and thought about this decision, and I've sought the counsel of godly advisors. So unless you say otherwise, I will choose, knowing that you are guiding me, and will trust you for the outcome. Thank you, Lord.

Your own ears will hear [the LORD]. Right behind you a voice will say, "This is the way you should go," whether to the right or to the left. ISAIAH 30:21

DAY 202 *Prayerful Moment*

A prayer about WORLDLINESS
When I want to change my world

JESUS,

Your followers must live *in* the world to change the world, but you don't want them to be *of* the world. That's a challenge. Please give me courage to engage with my culture while keeping me "safe from the evil one." I want to be different and to make a difference.

[Jesus prayed,] "I'm not asking you to take [my followers] out of the world, but to keep them safe from the evil one. They do not belong to this world any more than I do."
JOHN 17:15-16

DAY 203 *Prayerful Moment*

A prayer about COMPETITION
When I think about winning instead of serving

JESUS,

Your disciples argued about who would be the greatest in your Kingdom. I find that I also think about how I can impress you. I'm a competitive person, so I push myself to be first. That's dangerous in the Christian life. By worldly standards, you finished last—arrested, tortured, and executed. Yet I am to follow your example. Teach me the path of humility, of choosing last place and becoming a servant to others.

[Jesus] said, "Whoever wants to be first must take last place and be the servant of everyone else." MARK 9:35

A prayer about FREEDOM
When I feel constrained

DEAR GOD,

Ever since I was child, I have resisted restraints—wanting to be free, to make my own choices and go my own way. And I made a habit of pushing against the walls, testing the limits, especially during adolescence. I guess that's human nature—we don't want anyone telling us what we can and cannot do. For a while, I thought that you and the church were trying to limit my freedom with all the commandments, Bible teachings, and expectations. But the more I distanced myself from those "restraining" forces and pushed to be "free," the more I found myself enslaved to bad habits and outside pressures. Then I met Christ, the Truth, and he set me truly free. I am now free from the penalty and power of sin and free to choose right, to live in a way that honors you. I know you allow me the freedom to choose to sin, but I don't want to. And you've empowered me to be able to make godly, life-giving choices. Thank you, Lord, for setting me free.

You will know the truth, and the truth will set you free. . . .
So if the Son sets you free, you are truly free.
JOHN 8:32, 36

A prayer about PATIENCE
When I just can't wait

MY SAVIOR AND LORD,
I remember seeing a cartoon caption that read, "I want patience, and I want it now!" Unfortunately that describes my attitude most of the time. Patience is a virtue. It is also a fruit of the Spirit. But it certainly is not my default setting in life. I definitely do not like waiting. So I avoid the slow lane in traffic, expect the fast-food restaurant to be *fast*, and find it extremely frustrating to stand in a long line. I know this aspect of my personality helps me get things done—and quickly—but at times quality suffers, and I admit that some things take time to develop. I need a good dose of patience, Lord. Relationships can't be forced or rushed. And I realize that, just as with physical development, spiritual growth isn't instantaneous. Day by day—through challenges, conflicts, choices, relationships, and spiritual food and nurture—your Spirit continues to work in me, making me more and more like you, Jesus. I understand all this, but waiting is so difficult. So again, Savior, I pray for patience.

The Holy Spirit produces this kind of fruit in our lives: love, joy, peace, patience, kindness, goodness, faithfulness, gentleness, and self-control. GALATIANS 5:22-23

DAY 206

A prayer about HITTING THE WALL
When I have exhausted my resources

JESUS,
I have thought and expressed often that life is not a short sprint but a long-distance race, and I have tried to live that way, training, stretching, taking fluids, running the right pace, and more. But just as what often happens in a marathon, I have hit the wall. I have exhausted all my resources, and I am spent, gasping and wondering how I can take another step. Runners know that this experience is more than physical; the mind and emotions are totally involved. So I keep thinking about quitting—pulling out of all my activities, resigning from my responsibilities, and just putting life on hold. Maybe right now I need rest or nourishment. I know I need love and understanding . . . and direction. I'm not even sure what to pray for. You've been where I am—burdened, abandoned, and abused—yet you kept moving toward your calling, the Cross. O Lord, I'm amazed and overwhelmed that you continued to Calvary. Please reenergize me with renewed strength, gentle guidance, hope, and courage to finish the course you have laid out for me.

Take a new grip with your tired hands and strengthen your weak knees. Mark out a straight path for your feet so that those who are weak and lame will not fall but become strong. HEBREWS 12:12-13

DAY 207

A prayer about LIFE
When a loved one dies

DIVINE COMFORTER,

I feel like Martha at the tomb of her brother, Lazarus. I know death comes to everyone, but that knowledge doesn't ease the pain when I lose someone I care about. When an older person dies, we think, *She [or he] lived a good, long life*, as though that fact will somehow soften our grief. But that also doesn't help. At the news of death and then the funeral, I mourn the loss of all that person was and meant to others, especially me. I also mourn my own mortality, knowing that one day I will have to leave behind everyone and everything I have ever known. But we are in the land of the dying en route to the land of the living. That was Jesus' message to the grieving sisters. The reality of eternal life with you after death is the only remedy for my grief, the only hope for my time on earth. Thank you, Lord, for your comfort, your gift of eternal life, and your promise of heaven to come and a glorious reunion.

Jesus told [Martha], "I am the resurrection and the life. Anyone who believes in me will live, even after dying. Everyone who lives in me and believes in me will never ever die." JOHN 11:25-26

A prayer about CREATION
When I see the wonders in the world around me

O LORD MY GOD,
I am overwhelmed by the glorious beauty of your creation. Today we had "bad weather"—the forecasters were all over the situation with their charts, maps, and predictions—and it certainly made driving difficult. But even a powerful storm displays your might and design, especially when I consider how my local weather relates to others. I may be inconvenienced by the rain that a farmer needs. Winter snows provide protective cover in cold snaps and water in the spring. Even hurricanes play a part. So I lived my way through today's storm. Then tonight, after the skies cleared, I gazed upon the vast panoply of stars and was awestruck by your creativity and immensity—far beyond what I could ever imagine. You are amazing, God! Swallowtail butterflies, sunsets, golden leaves, the first shoot breaking through the earth, sparkling meandering rivers, rock formations, goldfinches, snow crystals, the sun's rays streaming through a prism, and the soft cry of a newborn all declare your glory. And to think that you love me!

When I look at the night sky and see the work of your fingers—the moon and the stars you set in place—what are mere mortals that you should think about them, human beings that you should care for them? Yet you made them only a little lower than God and crowned them with glory and honor. PSALM 8:3-5

DAY 209 *Prayerful Moment*

A prayer about ENCOURAGEMENT
When my spirits have been lifted by others

DEAR LORD,
Today I received an affirming, personal word from a friend. I was greatly encouraged. And the timing was perfect—I really needed those words. Thank you for the gift of my friend and the sincere message. You have told us to encourage one another. I want to be for others as my friend was to me—like Barnabas in the early church. Help me, Lord.

There was Joseph, the one the apostles nicknamed Barnabas (which means "Son of Encouragement"). ACTS 4:36

DAY 210 *Prayerful Moment*

A prayer about SACRIFICE
When my commitment costs me

LORD,
I hear the word *sacrifice* used in many contexts. Parents sacrifice for their children, workers for their companies, soldiers for their countries. These men and women forfeit freedom and privilege for a cause greater than themselves. No greater cause exists than to proclaim your name throughout the earth, and no cost is too great. Give me courage, Lord, to be willing to sacrifice everything for you.

[Paul said,] "For his sake I have discarded everything else, counting it all as garbage, so that I could gain Christ and become one with him." PHILIPPIANS 3:8-9

A prayer about LEGALISM
When I try to earn favor with God

HEAVENLY FATHER,
We love to keep score, to determine champions and also-rans. Usually those with the most points or achievements are pronounced winners. So I find myself comparing my works to others as though I'm in a game to win. That's not only unproductive but can be deadly in my spiritual life. I want to *win* in that contest and to be known as a spiritual person. And I'm afraid that my deeper motive is to gain favor with you, thinking you will love me more if I work harder and better in my religious responsibilities. I can easily laugh at the Pharisees, mocking their legalism and hypocrisy. But I act the same when I take pride in how well I keep your laws (and my additions to them) compared to others. Instead, I need to keep my eyes on Christ; remember that my salvation is all because of grace, not works; and understand that I can do nothing without your Spirit empowering me. Help me know that I should do good *because* you love me, not to earn your love.

If you are trying to make yourselves right with God by keeping the law, you have been cut off from Christ! You have fallen away from God's grace. GALATIANS 5:4

A prayer about AFFIRMATION

When I recognize my need to be noticed

O LORD,

On some days I feel just like a little kid looking for compliments and approval, wanting someone to notice my work or say how good I am. And not receiving any recognition or positive feedback can cause me to feel unloved, overlooked, and unappreciated—a real pity party. This often happens when I realize how tiny I am in this world, just one out of billions of people. Yet I know that you love me and that you shower me with your gifts and affirming words. As a flawed and sinful person, I deserve no praise or gifts, just condemnation. But by your grace you have chosen, forgiven, saved, and adopted me. When I focus on my failures and inadequacies, I feel small and insignificant. But when I think of your love for me, I feel like a child of the King. So please help me remember how much you care for me. And help me pass on your love to others, complimenting, noticing, encouraging—affirming them as your unique creations, made in your image, just as I am.

See how very much our Father loves us, for he calls us his children, and that is what we are! 1 JOHN 3:1

DAY 213

A prayer about ETERNITY
When I consider our infinite God

AWESOME GOD,

I cannot imagine anything eternal. The concept is far beyond what my limited human mind can conceive—that something has always been, before Creation and time, with no beginning—but I know that something must be "before." And I can't begin to conceive that something goes out and on forever, with no end, even though I know that something must continue, out there, far beyond my imagination. But that something is a Someone; it is you, eternal God. You have no beginning and no end. You are out there and in here—everywhere. You are unlimited in every way. I am so small and insignificant, less than a piece of cosmic dust in the universe, which itself is just a speck to you. Yet from eternity past you knew me and chose me as your own. And you love me! Who am I to resist your love? How could I ever think or act against your will? Yet I do—continually. I need to remember my place in your plan, Lord, for I am absolutely nothing without you.

All glory to him who alone is God, our Savior through Jesus Christ our Lord. All glory, majesty, power, and authority are his before all time, and in the present, and beyond all time! Amen. JUDE 1:25

DAY 214

A prayer about CHILDLIKE FAITH

When I become too "adult" in my relationship with God

DEAR FATHER,

Jesus taught that I should be like a child in my perspective and relationship with you. Open my eyes and my heart, Lord, to the faith and joy in the children all around me. When I watch a children's choir praising you in song, help me to notice the pure joy radiating from the faces of the little boys and girls as they raise their voices and hands. When I see small children at play in a park, running, laughing, and climbing, help me relish the way they embrace the day and their surroundings. Even when they take a spill, they don't stop for long. They run to their mothers, who bend down to hug them and dry their tears before sending them off to play again. What a contrast the zest of these children is to my usual tentative and cerebral approach to life. Help me know that I am your precious child and that you are watching every move, delighting with me in victories and celebrations, and hurting with me in defeats and pain. Hold me, Daddy.

Jesus said, "Let the children come to me. Don't stop them! For the Kingdom of Heaven belongs to those who are like these children." And he placed his hands on their heads and blessed them. MATTHEW 19:14-15

DAY 215

A prayer about ROAD RAGE
When I drive out of control

DEAR JESUS,

I have to admit—I was out of control this afternoon. Someone cut me off in traffic, forcing me to slam on my brakes and almost causing an accident. I was so angry that I sped up and got as close as I could to that car and was looking for a way to return the favor before I had to turn off. Traffic seems to bring out the worst in me, maybe because I'm always in a hurry or perhaps because I'm competitive and don't like to have drivers get ahead of me. Whatever the reason, I need to stay calm before I hurt myself and others. To make matters worse, I had a Christian sticker on my car; I can imagine the bad impression I was making for you, Lord. I pray for the discipline to start my travels earlier so I won't have to rush, and then perhaps even consider driving in the slow lane to avoid temptation. I say I want to live for you—what better place to start!

Stop being angry! Turn from your rage! Do not lose your temper—it only leads to harm. PSALM 37:8

DAY 216 *Prayerful Moment*

A prayer about BURNOUT
When I have reached the end of my energy

LORD,
I'm mentally and emotionally exhausted from dealing with complex issues, solving problems, and handling interruptions. Stressed, overwhelmed, burned out—I'm not sure how much more I can take. But when I read your Word, I realize that I have been doing everything in my own strength rather than depending on you. Help me trust you, Lord. And give me strength to soar.

Those who trust in the LORD will find new strength. They will soar high on wings like eagles. They will run and not grow weary. They will walk and not faint. ISAIAH 40:31

DAY 217 *Prayerful Moment*

A prayer about POWER
When I submit to God's sovereignty

SOVEREIGN GOD,
So much of the world revolves around power—political, economic, social, academic. But you are the almighty, sovereign, and all-powerful God. You created the universe, have caused nations to rise and fall, and have defeated Satan. And Lord, you have changed my life. I humbly submit to you, recognizing that I am powerless without you.

God is awesome in his sanctuary. The God of Israel gives power and strength to his people. Praise be to God!
PSALM 68:35

A prayer about PERSISTENCE
When I feel like giving up

JESUS,
When teaching your disciples about prayer, you said they should persist—"keep on asking . . . keep on seeking, and . . . keep on knocking." And I know that applies to other areas of the Christian life; you don't want us to get tired of doing good. Lately, I must admit, I've been tired and have been tempted to give up in certain areas of "doing good." Part of my problem is that I want to see results, and they just haven't been forthcoming. Continuing to reach out to someone, for example, gets discouraging without a show of spiritual interest. So I ask for the resolve to persist in acting in love. My prayer life has suffered as well. I know of so many needs and issues for which to pray, and I tend to want quick and obvious answers. Your statement that I should "keep on" tells me that eventually you will answer, but maybe not right away, and that the keeping on demonstrates faith and total reliance on you. Please give me that faith, Lord.

Keep on asking, and you will receive what you ask for. Keep on seeking, and you will find. Keep on knocking, and the door will be opened to you. For everyone who asks, receives. Everyone who seeks, finds. And to everyone who knocks, the door will be opened. LUKE 11:9-10

A prayer about SATISFACTION
When I don't feel fulfilled

HOLY SPIRIT,

You live in me and are transforming me to be more and more like Christ. You meet my most crucial need for salvation and also give me meaning and purpose for living. So why would I ever look elsewhere for satisfaction? But I do when I begin to believe the world's lies. Good advertisers know that first they have to create a feeling of dissatisfaction before presenting their "solution." Children see ads for toys and pester Mom and Dad for them; then, just days after being received with delight, the gifts lay discarded or broken. Parents become frustrated at their children's immaturity, but I often do the same, thinking that I *need* the new car or wardrobe or electronic wonder or romantic encounter to be happy and fulfilled. But that's a lie, and I should know better—because I know you. As David proclaimed, "Your unfailing love is better than life itself," and only you can satisfy. Please help me, Spirit of God, to resist the sales pitches and find my fulfillment in you and your will.

Your unfailing love is better than life itself; how I praise you! I will praise you as long as I live, lifting up my hands to you in prayer. You satisfy me more than the richest feast. I will praise you with songs of joy. PSALM 63:3-5

A prayer about WORKING FOR GOOD
When I consider "everything"

MY SOVEREIGN LORD,
You know that I love you. So I am claiming your promise in Romans and trusting you—that what I experienced today will in some way work "for the good." This verse is often quoted whenever a setback or tragedy occurs, and I've heard people try hard to find something good in a terrible situation. But as I reread this passage, the words *everything* and *together* jumped out. And I seemed to hear you explaining that I shouldn't isolate incidents and that you are weaving everything together for my *ultimate* good. In truth, you are sovereign and can do anything, even take a sinful act and use it in your plan, for your glory. So instead of trying to think positively about a negative situation, I need to simply trust you, remembering that you are perfect, holy, and righteous and that you love me and want only the very best for me. I am confident in my relationship with you: I am chosen, called, and your child, born again by grace through faith. I praise you, Lord.

We know that God causes everything to work together for the good of those who love God and are called according to his purpose for them. ROMANS 8:28

DAY 221

A prayer about SALVATION

When I think about what being saved means

MY LORD AND SAVIOR,

I have heard the term *saved* bandied about over the years, as in "I'm saved" or "Jesus saved me," and I have also used it casually. But the concept of salvation is most profound, and I dare not take it lightly. Lord, I know that I was lost—completely lost—separated from you, mired in sin, and headed straight to hell. I wasn't a good person who needed improving—though that's what most people probably thought of me—or even a bad person who needed reforming. I was sinful through and through, without hope. But because of the work of Christ alone, by grace alone, and through faith alone, you rescued me, declaring me "not guilty" and bound for heaven. You saved me from sin's penalty. You also saved me from sin's power. Before, my sinful nature controlled my attitude, thoughts, and actions. But you changed all that and are transforming me; thus, now I can choose to do what honors you. Salvation is not a cliché; it's true, real, and mine. Thank you, my Savior.

There is salvation in no one else! God has given no other name under heaven by which we must be saved.

ACTS 4:12

A prayer about INTEGRITY
When I want to be known for honesty

DEAR LORD,

I want to be a person of my word, one who acts with honesty and integrity in all that I do, in every area of life. I certainly cannot do this on my own—I need you. So please do your work in me and through me. In my relationships, integrity means telling the truth, being loyal, and refusing to belittle or gossip. In my job, it means putting in a full day's work for a day's pay, having a positive attitude, and doing my best. In my finances, it means not cheating merchants or customers, telling the truth on my tax forms, and meeting my obligations. In my relationship with you, it means being totally transparent, honest, and vulnerable; following you fully and sincerely; fulfilling my promises; and keeping our communication lines open and clear. Everyone who knows me—relatives, friends, church members, coworkers, neighbors, and more—should know that my "no" means no and my "yes" means yes. They should understand by watching me in action that I belong to you. This is my prayer, Lord.

I know, my God, that you examine our hearts and rejoice when you find integrity there. 1 CHRONICLES 29:17

DAY 223 *Prayerful Moment*

A prayer about TAKING RESPONSIBILITY
When the burden is on me

GOD,

When I am given an assignment, a task to accomplish, I want to do it well. Rather than make excuses or say it's someone else's responsibility, I need to step up to the challenge. Help me see each task as an opportunity to glorify you. And when I fail, give me the courage to admit what I did and take full responsibility for my actions.

A faithful, sensible servant is one to whom the master can give the responsibility of managing his other household servants and feeding them. MATTHEW 24:45

DAY 224 *Prayerful Moment*

A prayer about ENEMIES
When I feel surrounded

DEAR GOD,

I'm under assault—at least that's how I feel. At times the attacks are subtle. Often, however, they are direct, questioning my character, undermining my relationships, or mocking my faith. I feel like David, who cried out to you for help. I, too, trust you, Lord. I know that you love me and that Christ died for me. And through him I can live victoriously today. I will not be defeated!

I am trusting you, O LORD, saying, "You are my God!" My future is in your hands. Rescue me from those who hunt me down relentlessly. PSALM 31:14-15

A prayer about SAFETY
When I am concerned about people I love

DEAR GOD,

Recently I have been thinking about safety, with all the frustration, crime, and violence I see in the world. The fabric of society seems to be torn, the moral foundations crumbling. I am worried not so much about myself but about the people I love, especially the little ones. They are so defenseless against evil, Lord. In addition, adults who should be their protection are pulling back, leaving the weak exposed. Please watch over the children, God. Keep them safe; shield them from harm. Guide our political leaders; give them wisdom to know what they can do to stem violence and the courage to do it. With all the debate about guns, mental illness, laws, and related topics, help us understand that this is first of all a moral issue and that hearts must be changed. To that end, give me the opportunities, words, strength, and courage to speak up for the truths in your Word and to share the message of salvation through Christ. Though your Spirit, please empower me to be a reconciler and peacemaker for you.

This I declare about the LORD: He alone is my refuge, my place of safety; he is my God, and I trust him. For he will rescue you from every trap and protect you from deadly disease. He will cover you with his feathers. He will shelter you with his wings. His faithful promises are your armor and protection. PSALM 91:2-4

DAY 226

A prayer about CONFLICT

When I disagree with someone or someone disagrees with me

SOVEREIGN LORD,

I tend to be a conflict avoider. But that leads to superficial conversations and shallow relationships. At times, I have allowed friends and others to make light of my strongly held beliefs. Today I was silent when I should have said something in response to an outrageous statement. I withdrew when I should have engaged because I knew what would transpire—one word leading to another and then anger or awkward silence. I know conflict is part of life: people will disagree and argue—all relationships have those moments. I also confess, however, that in a confrontation when I am the one being confronted, I often shut out the other person, becoming defensive and responding irrationally. I pray for vulnerability, Lord, to be open when a loved one speaks truth to me. I also pray for wisdom, Father, to know when to join the fray and when to back off, to know what to say and how to say it. Help me to state my case, to speak the truth with love, to disagree without being disagreeable.

Pride leads to conflict; those who take advice are wise.

PROVERBS 13:10

DAY 227

A prayer about FINISHING STRONG
When I begin to tire in life's race

DEAR GOD,

A marathon runner needs conditioning, nourishment, resolve, and encouragement. Anyone can buy nice running shoes and shorts, cheer at the starting gun, and take off quickly with a flourish. But many quickly tire and slow to nearly a crawl. Others exhaust all their resources, convince themselves that they can't take another step, and quit. Still others limp through the last half and barely get to the end. The Christian "race" seems to follow a similar pattern. I have seen many who began with energy, enthusiasm, and optimism. Eventually, however, these same "runners" struggle, limp along, or drop out. I don't want to be one of the casualties, Lord. But even if I can see the end in sight, I don't want to merely survive and settle for just making it to the end. I want to finish well, strong—enduring, yes, but giving everything I have, my all, as I stretch for the line and enter eternity, the heavenly prize, with joy. I want to make a difference while I live. Please empower, motivate, and uphold me, Lord.

I focus on this one thing: Forgetting the past and looking forward to what lies ahead, I press on to reach the end of the race and receive the heavenly prize for which God, through Christ Jesus, is calling us. PHILIPPIANS 3:13-14

A prayer about EXCELLENCE
When I set a standard for my life

LORD,

I like cruise control in my car because driving seems easier, but this automotive convenience can put me in danger if I'm not paying attention. I can also put life on cruise control. That's easy to do—not too complicated; it usually means doing just enough to get by at work, at church, in responsibilities and assignments, in relationships . . . in life. Usually living that way doesn't happen by choice; I simply drift into a comfortable mode and pace. Then, if I'm not careful, I begin to settle for *average* effort, mediocre work, and okay behavior, certainly not stretching to accomplish more than what is required. But you desire much more than simply a passing grade, just getting by. You expect my *best* effort in every area, demanding excellence, especially in worship, values, and morality. So I don't want to fall short and settle for anything less. Others may be satisfied with lesser goals and standards, but I represent you. Give me strength to not "settle" and to move beyond good and better to best—God-honoring excellence.

Supplement your faith with a generous provision of moral excellence, and moral excellence with knowledge, and knowledge with self-control, and self-control with patient endurance, and patient endurance with godliness, and godliness with brotherly affection, and brotherly affection with love for everyone. 2 PETER 1:5-7

DAY 229

A prayer about being FEARFULLY AND WONDERFULLY MADE

When I see the miracle that is me

BLESSED CREATOR,
I am a miracle. I don't say that in a prideful way, but I simply acknowledge your work in my life, from conception till now. You formed me, "knit me together," made me what I am. Every baby is an amazing testimony to your presence in this world, your creativity, and your power. Eyes, ears, tiny fingers and toes complete with nails; the lungs, heart, and other internal organs; the brain and nervous system; and little cries, quivering lips, and flailing arms—everything is working at that grand entrance into the world as a new life is entrusted to parents. That child will eventually walk, run, sing, dance, swim, write, read, draw. I, too, am unique, and I am yours. When I consider my senses, my physical abilities, my mind—to think and create—and my emotions, I realize how wonderfully complex you made me. And the most profound truth—you created me in your image. I worship and adore you. I love you, my Creator, my Father, my Savior.

You made all the delicate, inner parts of my body and knit me together in my mother's womb. Thank you for making me so wonderfully complex! Your workmanship is marvelous—how well I know it. You watched me as I was being formed in utter seclusion, as I was woven together in the dark of the womb. PSALM 139:13-15

DAY 230 *Prayerful Moment*

A prayer about HUMILITY
When I begin to think too highly of myself

O GOD,
I did it again. Just when I think I'm making great strides in the Christian life, I stumble. This time pride knocked me down. I felt so good about what I had accomplished that I began to feel full of myself. And when I didn't get credit, I pouted. Forgive me, Lord. Help me remember that my good works are for *your* glory, not mine. I want to be your humble servant.

You rescue the humble, but your eyes watch the proud and humiliate them. 2 SAMUEL 22:28

DAY 231 *Prayerful Moment*

A prayer about ENJOYING GOD
When I remember all that God has done

HEAVENLY FATHER,
According to the Westminster Shorter Catechism, "Man's chief end is to glorify God and to enjoy him forever." I think I understand the "glorify" and "forever" parts, but I wonder at times how I can enjoy you. Help me remember your love, forgiveness, guidance, gifts, promises, and care. I want to live joyfully, Father, so I will sing your praises, exult in your presence, and rejoice in my salvation.

See, God has come to save me. I will trust in him and not be afraid. The LORD GOD is my strength and my song; he has given me victory. ISAIAH 12:2

DAY 232

A prayer about PRESSURE
When I am feeling pressed in on every side

DEAR GOD,
Today I have been feeling tremendous pressure from all sides. Some of this comes from my own expectations for my performance. I want to complete assignments on time and achieve results of the highest quality. So I pray that you'd help me be able to cut myself some slack and take things one at a time. But I'm also feeling pressure from other sources. My schedule is jammed with events and appointments that require my presence and full attention. In addition, some family members expect me to act a certain way, even if I don't feel like it. And a number of bills and other financial obligations are taxing my dwindling resources. I also feel pulled to those tempting indulgences that aren't good for me as a way to cope. I would ask you to remove these pressures, Lord, but you know what is best. So instead, I pray for the inner strength to withstand the external forces, relying completely on you to work through me to answer the questions and meet the demands.

If you fail under pressure, your strength is too small.
PROVERBS 24:10

DAY 233

A prayer about EMPATHY

When I interact with someone in need

FATHER,

Today a friend was sharing a story of personal need. This friend was bothered, visibly upset. I stopped what I was doing and gave the appearance of listening—leaning in, nodding appropriately, and even saying, "Uh-huh." But that was phony; I was thinking about my next conversation, other tasks on my to-do list, and how much time the conversation was consuming. That seems to be a tendency for me lately—I'm so preoccupied with my own needs and schedule that I cannot see or hear anyone else. I don't like it when I act that way, and I know that you don't either. As I read the Bible, I see how Jesus took time to reach out and relate to each person. Help me remember to pray for the person as I speak, to look my friend in the eye, and to really listen. Give me feelings like yours, genuine empathy for the individual. I want to be known as someone who truly cares about others, not to enhance my reputation but to help them and to glorify you.

All of you should be of one mind. Sympathize with each other. Love each other as brothers and sisters. Be tenderhearted, and keep a humble attitude. 1 PETER 3:8

DAY 234

A prayer about CONTENTMENT
When dissatisfaction sets in

DEAR LORD JESUS,

Several times today I felt frustrated with my current situation, as though I was somehow being shortchanged. A TV ad caught my imagination as it promoted a "must have" product—a labor-saving device, the newest electronic toy, or something even bigger like an exotic trip or a new car. I learned about a friend's latest adventure, exciting promotion at work, or new all-the-bells-and-whistles possession. *I should do or have that,* I thought. *That should be me!* I fantasized a different life from what I am currently living and desired *more* of whatever good I now have. The apostle Paul experienced all sides—everything and nothing, up and down, in-crowd member and outsider, the heights of academic and spiritual acclaim and the depths of torture and prison, yet he could be content in *every* situation . . . because he found his life in you. Please give me that secret of contentment, Savior. Help me know that all I need is you.

I have learned how to be content with whatever I have. I know how to live on almost nothing or with everything. I have learned the secret of living in every situation, whether it is with a full stomach or empty, with plenty or little.

PHILIPPIANS 4:11-12

DAY 235

A prayer about my REPUTATION
When I wonder what others think of me

FATHER,

I am convinced that a good reputation is important. Unfortunately, after a person is branded with a bad one, such as "cheater," "liar," or "unreliable," the label can be difficult to shake. No wonder the proverb says that being well thought of is better than being wealthy. I have been thinking about the self-portrait I have been presenting. I am concerned because I know that what others think of me reflects on you, for I have been outspoken about my allegiance to you. I would hate to have someone say, "Well, if that's what a Christian is like, then I'm not interested!" I want to be like Jesus and to reflect his values, humility, focus, love, and selfless service. I desire to be known as one who is loyal, faithful, honest, truthful, disciplined, moral, joyful, encouraging, and most of all, committed to Christ. And I want these qualities to be true of me, not simply an image I am trying to project. Please help me, Lord.

Choose a good reputation over great riches; being held in high esteem is better than silver or gold. PROVERBS 22:1

DAY 236

A prayer about MEMORIES

When I remember people and events in my past

HEAVENLY FATHER,

Remembering affects me in several ways. Often when I least expect it, a calendar date or a specific place triggers a painful memory of an event that caused conflict or grief. At other times, I recall happy occasions, especially when reunited with family and friends whom I haven't seen recently. Usually a high school reunion evokes both feelings. I admit, Lord, that sometimes I wish I could return to a certain era—a time and place where life was uncomplicated and I felt loved. (Of course, I conveniently forget the difficulties that seemed overwhelming back then.) I can do the same with romance, idealizing a past relationship and thinking, *What if* . . . Thank you, Father, for my history, especially those people and events you used to bring me closer to you. Thank you for the challenges that taught me valuable life lessons. And most of all, thank you for calling me and transforming me by your Spirit. For that memory I am eternally grateful. I value past memories as I live in the present, for you.

I have tried to stimulate your wholesome thinking and refresh your memory. I want you to remember what the holy prophets said long ago and what our Lord and Savior commanded through your apostles. 2 PETER 3:1-2

DAY 237 *Prayerful Moment*

A prayer about PEACEMAKING
When I need to mediate a conflict

JESUS,

Peacemaking is not my strength. In fact, I try to avoid conflict. However, I have been asked to help resolve a dispute between two people I care about. I'm not good at this—please help me. Give me strength to move forward, words to say, and courage to speak the truth. And I pray for each "combatant" in the conflict. May they see the other's perspective, act in love, and work for a peaceful resolution. I put it all in your hands, dear Savior.

God blesses those who work for peace, for they will be called the children of God. MATTHEW 5:9

DAY 238 *Prayerful Moment*

A prayer about MONEY
When I evaluate my focus on finances

ETERNAL GIFT GIVER,

I know money itself isn't bad, but the *love* of money leads to "all kinds of evil." Yet I find myself chasing the almighty dollar. Money doesn't buy happiness, but it opens many doors and opportunities. Help me be a good steward so I can invest in the Kingdom.

The love of money is the root of all kinds of evil. And some people, craving money, have wandered from the true faith and pierced themselves with many sorrows.
1 TIMOTHY 6:10

A prayer about RENEWAL
When I am sliding spiritually

DIVINE COMFORTER,
I have been in a spiritual rut, going through the motions but without any passion. No great commandment breaking has brought me to this place, not even a series of small infractions—just the daily and regular routines of life. Slowly, over the weeks and months, I slid to where I am today. The process was so gradual that I didn't notice . . . until lately. I've heard someone say, "If you're not as close to God as you were, guess who moved," with the obvious answer—"You!" That certainly has been true for me. Forgive me, Lord, for my soul neglect. I want to be near you, sensitive to your leading, aware of your presence, feeling your power, and seeing you work in and through me. I am a sinner, so my natural tendency is to pull away. But at conversion, you changed me, giving me a new nature. So I humbly submit to you, Holy Spirit. Do your restoration work in me. Stop my wayward movement, revive my spirit, and pull me close. Renew me.

Let the Spirit renew your thoughts and attitudes. Put on your new nature, created to be like God—truly righteous and holy. EPHESIANS 4:23-24

DAY 240

A prayer about THANKSGIVING

When I consider and count all my blessings

FATHER,

Thinking back over the day, I feel overwhelmed by your goodness. You have given so much, for which I am profoundly thankful. Often I take your blessings for granted, either not recognizing them or somehow expecting your gifts as though I deserve them. Please forgive me. Now as I remember your blessings, I thank you for life itself, for the ability to breathe, and for my senses, to experience your world. Thank you for your provision and care, protection, healing, and sustenance. I am safeguarded by police officers, firefighters, and more. I have financial resources, food, a place to live, and doctors and hospitals nearby. Thank you for loved ones and other relationships—friends, neighbors, coworkers—with whom I interact and from whom I learn. I thank you for my brothers and sisters in Christ and for my church, especially those who preach and teach and serve. And, most of all, thank you for sending Jesus to die for me, for forgiving me, and for giving me eternal life by grace through faith. I love you, Lord.

You prepare a feast for me in the presence of my enemies. You honor me by anointing my head with oil. My cup overflows with blessings. PSALM 23:5

A prayer about CULTURE WARS
When my values clash with those of the world

DEAR JESUS,

You are perfect, and when you lived on earth, you did everything right—no mistakes, no slipups, no errors, no sins. Yet you were misunderstood, slandered, hated, betrayed, deserted, despised, and rejected. Just before facing the fate you knew awaited, you explained to the disciples that your followers also would have trouble in the world because we, too, would be at odds with societal norms and conventional wisdom. You warned that we would face opposition and persecution for following you. I felt that today, and every day your prediction is being fulfilled for me. Daily life seems like a war zone as I am assaulted with contrary values, morals, and beliefs. I see a growing gap between how you want me to live and what is pictured as a "normal" lifestyle. And I feel increasingly marginalized and ostracized. Please give me the courage to stand for your truth in a society of relativism, to hold to biblical morality in a culture of hedonism, and to proclaim, with love and despite the personal consequences, that you are the *only* way.

[Jesus said,] "If the world hates you, remember that it hated me first. The world would love you as one of its own if you belonged to it, but you are no longer part of the world. I chose you to come out of the world, so it hates you."
JOHN 15:18-19

A prayer about VALUES
When I realize what is most important

HEAVENLY FATHER,
Jesus spoke about seeking your Kingdom above everything else in the context of highlighting your abundant provision for us and the importance of not being consumed by worry. People can allow the concerns of everyday life—important matters such as food, clothing, and shelter—to push you out of your rightful place in their lives. Sometimes a relationship takes priority over you. Every now and then a personal goal or dream takes top spot. Even church responsibilities, programs, and activities can intrude. But mostly the normal stresses and pressures of daily living consume my attention. At such times, when I scurry around to get something done, it's all I think about. Forgive me, Lord. I also confess that I don't seek you *first* when I meet a challenge—usually only as a last resort. O Father, I want *all* my values to be holy and right, but I desperately desire seeking you and your Kingdom to stand above all else.

Seek the Kingdom of God above all else, and live righteously, and he will give you everything you need. MATTHEW 6:33

A prayer about SILENCE AND SOLITUDE
When I need time alone with God

LORD ABOVE,

Elijah courageously defied Ahab and Jezebel, confronted the prophets of Baal, and claimed a mighty victory for you. But in the aftermath he was hungry, exhausted, and afraid. When I read this story, I am struck by how you got his attention and then ministered to him. After the windstorm, the earthquake, and the fire, you spoke with a "gentle whisper." Elijah had heard you earlier because you had told him to go to the mountain to meet you. But in the whisper you brought healing and hope. Like Elijah, I typically look for you in the wind—usually great preaching and teaching; the earthquake—powerful events; and fire—emotional gatherings. But at times you want to whisper to me. And for me to hear you, I should be alone with you . . . in a quiet place. You know this isn't easy for me to do, but I need your voice now, Lord, in intimate conversation. As I pull away from my busy schedule and noisy world, please calm my troubled spirit and speak to me.

After the wind there was an earthquake, but the LORD was not in the earthquake. And after the earthquake there was a fire, but the LORD was not in the fire. And after the fire there was the sound of a gentle whisper. When Elijah heard it, he wrapped his face in his cloak and went out and stood at the entrance of the cave. And a voice said, "What are you doing here, Elijah?" 1 KINGS 19:11-13

DAY 244 *Prayerful Moment*

A prayer about MARGIN
When I feel overwhelmed

DEAR LORD GOD,
I'm frazzled. I feel as though I have been running all day—driving, talking, meeting, planning, calling, spending . . . stressing. This has become my daily routine, my way of life. I need margin—space and time to think, to read the Word, and to spend with you. Calm me, Father. Fill me with your Spirit, your peace, your assurance. Help me to take a deep breath and relax in your loving arms.

Those who live in the shelter of the Most High will find rest in the shadow of the Almighty. PSALM 91:1

DAY 245 *Prayerful Moment*

A prayer about RESPECT
When I perceive people as God does

DEAR LORD,
I need both respect and love. I want to be accepted for who I am, valued, and affirmed. Since that's what I want for myself, I should do the same for others. So please give me eyes to see people as you see them, each one your special creation with dignity and worth. Help me treat all people with care, no matter how they act.

Do to others whatever you would like them to do to you. This is the essence of all that is taught in the law and the prophets. MATTHEW 7:12

DAY 246

A prayer about POPULARITY

When I want to be liked by everyone

DEAR JESUS,

I admit that I like to be liked, and the more people who like me, the better I feel. I suppose this is normal; no one enjoys being *dis*liked. But sometimes this popularity need gets in the way of values that should be much more important, the main one being to glorify you in all that I do. Forgive me, Lord, for being, at times, like the Pharisees who "loved human praise more than the praise of God." I remember, Jesus, that you drew massive crowds who wanted something from you. But you weren't interested in being popular, just in doing your Father's will. And you were ultimately abandoned and condemned, "despised and rejected," as Isaiah predicted. Give me the strength, I pray, to be willing to lose the crowd, to stand alone, to be despised . . . for you. I know that being close to you might distance me from my friends. But I am willing to pay that price. Human praise means nothing—only God's praise is worth seeking. Following you is all that matters to me.

They loved human praise more than the praise of God.
JOHN 12:43

DAY 247

A prayer about GOD MOMENTS

When I have a divine encounter

DEAR JESUS,

Wow! What a special, unexpected gift and a dramatic answer to prayer. What happened can only be described as a "God thing," "God sighting," or "God moment." Thank you, Jesus. Actually, I'm not sure why I was so surprised when it happened; after all, I have asked often for your guidance and divine intervention. And in your Word you have promised to always be with me. Why am I so easily lulled into complacency in my relationship with you? Why do I doubt and exclaim, "I can't believe it!" when you come through? I should stand amazed and humbled every day! Forgive me, Lord, for being insensitive to what you do for me all day. In truth, you are continually giving me those "moments," but I have not been "sighting" them. Open my heart and my eyes that I might see you and your marvelous deeds. I know you love me and are constantly acting on my behalf. Thank you. I want to live in confidence, knowing that you are with me, upholding me, and working for me.

O LORD my God, you have performed many wonders for us. Your plans for us are too numerous to list. You have no equal. If I tried to recite all your wonderful deeds, I would never come to the end of them. PSALM 40:5

DAY 248

A prayer about CORRECTION
When I need to be set straight

DEAR LORD,

I love your Word. Thank you for the ancient Scriptures—History, Prophecy, Poetry, Gospels, and Epistles—inspired by the Holy Spirit, faithfully recorded by chosen writers, and handed down from generation to generation. You gave the Bible to reveal your person and plan . . . and to change lives. One of the most personal outcomes from reading and studying your Word happens when you point out to me where I am going wrong and push me back to the right path. As I journey through life, I am easily distracted and can venture away from the way I should go, so I need your firm guidance. And that comes when I'm reading a passage, and the Spirit begins to convict me of my sin and show me what I need to do. At times your correction is difficult and painful, and I resist. But I know your way is best. I yield, Lord, to you and your perfect will. I promise to read and study the Bible, listen to your messages, and take steps to correct my ways.

I have hidden your word in my heart, that I might not sin against you. PSALM 119:11

DAY 249

A prayer about WORRY

When concerns about tomorrow interrupt my sleep tonight

DEAR LORD,

I admit that I worry easily, about virtually everything: tasks undone, potential problems, physical health, strained relationships, financial challenges . . . even politics and weather. A news report, a casual comment from a friend, a less-than-spectacular medical report, or an impending deadline or responsibility can cause my mind to spin and my emotions to shift into high gear. And as you know, these worries can almost consume my thoughts and keep me tossing and turning or staring at the ceiling well past my bedtime. I know in my head that you are in control and that you love me and that you have promised to give me everything I need. Please help me to know this in my heart, to truly believe all those truths. Give me insight, I pray, into how to manage these situations as they come in ways that glorify you. And please calm my spirit, helping me to relax and rest in you, trusting that you are providing for me right now and during the night and will continue to do so tomorrow.

Seek the Kingdom of God above all else, and live righteously, and he will give you everything you need. So don't worry about tomorrow, for tomorrow will bring its own worries. Today's trouble is enough for today. MATTHEW 6:33-34

A prayer about UNDERSTANDING
When I am confused about Scripture

PRECIOUS SAVIOR,

While you taught on this earth, you gathered a wide variety of people, from the obsessively religious to the completely secular. You promised the disciples that you would give understanding to everyone who truly listened to your teaching. I admit that sometimes my heart isn't open when I peruse Scripture. Instead, I am reading to just cross another daily Bible reading off my list. Forgive me. I want to hear you. Please speak to me and increase my understanding. And please keep me from being like the Pharisees, who used Scripture against others and to bolster their own position, taking your words out of context. They pretended to listen, but their ears and minds were closed. I am a novice at Bible study, but I want to grow in understanding the Word. Lead me to godly teachers and mature believers who can help me learn of you. And for those passages that seem too difficult for me, give me patience and insight as your Spirit illuminates them.

[Jesus'] disciples came and asked him, "Why do you use parables when you talk to the people?" He replied, "You are permitted to understand the secrets of the Kingdom of Heaven, but others are not. To those who listen to my teaching, more understanding will be given, and they will have an abundance of knowledge. But for those who are not listening, even what little understanding they have will be taken away from them." MATTHEW 13:10-12

DAY 251 *Prayerful Moment*

A prayer about SPIRITUAL LIFE SKILLS
When I desire to know and serve God better

LORD,
I have learned many "how tos" of life. But I have neglected to learn all the spiritual life skills I need. When the disciples asked Jesus to teach them how to pray, he answered with the Lord's Prayer. Please lead me to those who can teach me more about how to worship, give, pray, apply Scripture, explain what I believe, and serve. And please give me opportunities to teach these vital skills to other believers.

Once Jesus was in a certain place praying. As he finished, one of his disciples came to him and said, "Lord, teach us to pray, just as John taught his disciples." LUKE 11:1

DAY 252 *Prayerful Moment*

A prayer about NEW LIFE
When I see the changes that God has made in me

HOLY SPIRIT,
What a difference you have made. I have been transformed into an entirely new person. Some people can point to radical change, from sinner to saint, night to day—not so with me. I was considered a good person. I knew better, of course, but I wasn't "terrible." Yet I was totally lost without you. Since trusting Christ as Savior, I am "found" and new. Thank you, Lord!

Anyone who belongs to Christ has become a new person. The old life is gone; a new life has begun! 2 CORINTHIANS 5:17

A prayer about PROVISION
When I understand my needs and God's supply

DEAR LORD,

I recognize that I have wants and needs and that I sometimes confuse the two. Needs are crucial for survival, but most of my wants are extras that I think I must have. My body needs oxygen, water, and nutrients. I also need clothing and shelter to protect me from the elements and other potential dangers. You made me as a social creature, so relationships are vital—family, friends, community. Transportation, health care, and financial resources might also be on that list. Then I consider my spiritual needs. Every person has a hole in the soul that only you can fill—I need you. You have promised to provide all I need, and you do so much more. As a frail human being, I need direction and guidance, and you lead me. In my struggles, conflicts, and sorrows, I need assurance, answers, and comfort, which you generously provide. And you give eternal life, my most profound need. Thank you, Lord, for your provision, and keep me from those irrelevant, superfluous desires that tempt me away from trusting you.

God will generously provide all you need. Then you will always have everything you need and plenty left over to share with others. 2 CORINTHIANS 9:8

A prayer about LETTING GO

When I hold on too tightly

MY LORD,

I need to move on, to let go of the past and live in the present, preparing for the future. This seems to be a difficult process for me, and I'm not sure why. Maybe because times are tough and my problems are complex with no solutions in sight, I yearn for an idealized past. Or perhaps I just find the act of letting go difficult. I can hold on in relationships, too. I remember wanting my parents to let me grow up. But now I can hold others back, seeing them as immature or refusing to forgive a past offense. This reveals my lack of trust in you, Lord. I need to release and move on. Please forgive me. The world doesn't depend on me, but on you. I know you are good and you love me, so I need to trust you with each step forward, for my happiness and security. I need to hold everything—relationships, possessions, finances, dreams—very loosely, ready to release them at the right time. Give me the resolve and strength to let go.

Remember what happened to Lot's wife! If you cling to your life, you will lose it, and if you let your life go, you will save it.
LUKE 17:32-33

A prayer about FRIENDS
When I think about my dearest relationships

HEAVENLY FATHER,
Extroverts seem to thrive on relationships and have many friends. Introverts seem to need breaks between interpersonal interactions. I'm not sure where I fit because I have both tendencies. At times I'd rather get away from everyone and just be alone. But I also need close relationships, people outside of family who care about me, whom I can hang with and confide in. I am blessed with friends who know me and want to be with me. And right now, I pray for them by name. These people listen to me and pray for me. Sometimes they push back on my ideas and choices, helping me stay on course. Your Word gives many examples of friends, both good (David and Jonathan) and not so good (Job's friends). And you've said that a *real* friend "sticks closer than a brother." Thank you for the real friends in my life; they stay with me in all circumstances, despite my mistakes and foibles, and they speak truth to me. Please help me be that kind of friend to them.

There are "friends" who destroy each other, but a real friend sticks closer than a brother. PROVERBS 18:24

DAY 256

A prayer about ANSWERS TO PRAYER

When I know God hears and cares

HEAVENLY FATHER,

Prayer is a normal part of my life, my daily routine. I pray often—in the morning, in church, in the evening (like now), in a quick response to the prayer chain, at meals, in difficulties, and many other times. I admit that most of my prayers are filled with requests, everything from healing for a friend to finding something I've lost. I can come to you anytime with my thoughts, feelings, worship, and requests because Jesus opened the way. Thank you, Lord. I am confident that you hear me, even when my prayers are simply silent, heavenward thoughts. And I know you answer my prayers, everything I think, whisper, or shout—big and small. The answers can be "no," "yes," or "wait"—but you *do* answer. I have experienced your yeses through the years, sometimes in dramatic fashion. Actually every breath is a gift, an answer to my prayer. You are amazing, God. I can hardly grasp the fact that you know me, love me, and care about me—and you listen and answer. Thank you, Father.

You faithfully answer our prayers with awesome deeds, O God our savior. PSALM 65:5

A prayer about ABILITIES

When I recognize how God has enabled me to do his work

DEAR LORD,

I know I have certain talents, strengths, and gifts. I was born with many of them; others have been developed through the years. Some of these abilities are obvious and others hidden, by choice or by their nature. Today I was able to use a mix of those abilities to accomplish an important task and to help others. At times, I think I have nothing to offer, especially when comparing myself to those who seem much more gifted—at least it seems that way. I may even begin to feel sorry for myself and wish that I could be like someone else. So I can easily get caught up in myself and forget that you created me the way I am, that you have equipped me with "gifts for doing certain things well" and empowered me to make a difference in the world. Forgive me for thinking less of your creation and for wishing I were different. Thank you for making me uniquely who I am. And help me to use all that I am to glorify you.

In his grace, God has given us different gifts for doing certain things well. So if God has given you the ability to prophesy, speak out with as much faith as God has given you. If your gift is serving others, serve them well. If you are a teacher, teach well. ROMANS 12:6-7

DAY 258 *Prayerful Moment*

A prayer about CHOICES

When I face an important decision

HEAVENLY FATHER,

When Joshua confronted your people at a turning point in their history, he plainly stated his challenge: "Choose today whom you will serve." Every day I face similar choices where I can move toward the idols of this world or stay focused on you. With Joshua, I declare, "As for me and my family, we will serve the LORD."

Choose today whom you will serve. . . . But as for me and my family, we will serve the LORD.

JOSHUA 24:15

DAY 259 *Prayerful Moment*

A prayer about APPLYING SCRIPTURE

When I need to put biblical truth into practice

FATHER GOD,

I have read the Bible for a long time and know many of its major teachings. I have also memorized verses. But living for you means more than knowing; it also involves being and doing—allowing your Word to change my life. Help me to listen more carefully when your Spirit illuminates a passage and to put into practice your truth. Show me how to *live* your Word each day.

Don't just listen to God's word. You must do what it says.

JAMES 1:22

DAY 260

A prayer about EXAMPLE
When I need to make a good impression

HEAVENLY FATHER,
If asked, I would readily admit that I am a Christian, a "Christ-one," someone who claims Jesus as Savior and Lord. In fact, I have given my testimony several times in Christian settings and attend church regularly, for worship, education, Bible studies, and many other events. Beyond that, however, how do I make known my identification with Christ and his Kingdom? Do I effectively imitate your Son in how I think—my values, perspective, hopes, and thought life? Do people know about you by the way I speak, relate, and act? I know this is a challenge because of the kind of world I live in and the pressures I feel and face, but I want to be your person. Whether I am relatively old (like Paul) or young (like Timothy), many people—believers and unbelievers—are observing me and drawing conclusions about the reality of my faith by how well I reflect your character and values. Help me to model maturity in faith, to be a good example. May people see Christ in me and be drawn to him!

Don't let anyone think less of you because you are young. Be an example to all believers in what you say, in the way you live, in your love, your faith, and your purity.
1 TIMOTHY 4:12

DAY 261

A prayer about TRUTH
When I point people to the Savior

DEAR JESUS,
Many people today assert that absolute truth does not exist, that each person has his or her own—everything is relative. They may say, "Well, if that works for you, good, but it's not for me." Others believe in truth as a concept but don't think anyone can know it or find it. Yet all are seeking answers, meaning, and purpose. Truth means reality, fact, certainty. A reliable standard allows us to know how far off we are, and these days society is *way* off the mark. You told the disciples that you are the Truth. Later you stood before the one who would condemn you to death and told him the truth. Those who know you are set free from error and sin and death, and they know what is true. O Savior, my heart aches for those who turn away. They have heard and seen the truth, but they reject it. Use me, I pray, to lovingly point them to you and break through their philosophical haze that wants to debate instead of believing in you.

Pilate said, "So you are a king?" Jesus responded, "You say I am a king. Actually, I was born and came into the world to testify to the truth. All who love the truth recognize that what I say is true." "What is truth?" Pilate asked.
JOHN 18:37-38

A prayer about PROCRASTINATION
When I put off doing what I know I should

DEAR LORD,

According to Isaac Newton, one of your natural laws is "inertia"—the tendency of something to remain at rest (or in motion) unless acted upon by an outside force. I certainly can identify with the "at rest" tendency. With a task or assignment that I find even the least bit unpleasant or uncomfortable, I can find numerous excuses for not getting out of my chair and doing it. And I admit that I have done this with some of the actions that you want me to take. I am more comfortable in my home than out in the community or mission field. I feel more threatened talking with my neighbors or strangers than with friends and family. And serving at church takes time and effort. I can even procrastinate spending time with you in the Word and prayer, choosing television instead. I don't want to be that kind of person, Lord. Remind me daily that Jesus left heaven to become a baby; he gave himself to others; he submitted to human authorities; he took up his cross and climbed Calvary.

Don't put it off; do it now! Don't rest until you do.
PROVERBS 6:4

A prayer about SELF-CONTROL
When I need restraint

HOLY SPIRIT,
According to Galatians 5:23, self-control is a fruit of the Spirit, a by-product of your work in me. And that's exactly what I need. Whether the issue is eating, drinking, talking, driving, reacting to an insult or injustice, expressing feelings, or acting in anger, I need you to restrain my natural impulse to go over the top. When I lose control, I lose the battle and damage relationships, often irreparably. I become someone I don't want to be. In a disagreement, my overreaction quickly moves the focus off the topic and onto me, what I have said or the way I am acting. Sometimes I whip off an angry e-mail or use hateful words—in both cases, actions that I quickly regret. I want to be a disciplined person who keeps body, mind, and emotions in check. My deepest desire is to do *everything*, in public or private, for your glory, and only you can give me self-control.

A person without self-control is like a city with broken-down walls. PROVERBS 25:28

A prayer about LIVING SACRIFICE
When I need to be totally devoted to God

HOLY SPIRIT,

Paul told believers in Rome to give their bodies to God as a "living and holy sacrifice," and those words speak to us, too. I know what a *sacrifice* is, Lord, because the Old Testament is filled with rules and stories about your people offering lambs, bulls, and other animals in sacred ceremonies. But on all those occasions, the animals died, their blood spilled on the altar. I also know that Jesus gave his life as the final sacrifice for sin as he died on the cross. Here, however, I read that you want me to be a *living* sacrifice. My interpretation is that I should be fully alive to you but dead to sin and totally devoted to your service. I can easily say that I am yours, but so often I don't act that way. Instead, I go my own way, similar to a lamb that jumps off the altar and runs away. So again, I give you all of me, beginning with my body. I know this is the only way to live. Please transform me into a new person.

Dear brothers and sisters, I plead with you to give your bodies to God because of all he has done for you. Let them be a living and holy sacrifice—the kind he will find acceptable. This is truly the way to worship him. ROMANS 12:1

DAY 265 *Prayerful Moment*

A prayer about WARNINGS
When I should proceed with caution

GOD,

The red flags are waving and the caution lights are flashing. Your Word gives many warnings because you love people and want them to take the way that leads to life: "Stay away from this!" "Do not go here!" "This way leads to death." Instead of taking your words seriously, we move on full speed, to our peril. No wonder the world is in such bad shape. Help me heed your warnings, Lord, to carefully follow your instructions for living.

How I hated discipline! If only I had not ignored all the warnings! PROVERBS 5:12

DAY 266 *Prayerful Moment*

A prayer about SADNESS
When I am feeling blue

FATHER,

I'm not sure what's wrong, but I can't shake this feeling of sadness. Maybe the cause is as simple as the gloomy weather or just needing sleep. But I don't like living with a sense of despondency. O Father, pull me close in your loving arms. Whisper words of love and hope. Turn my gaze from myself to you. I love you, Lord. Please restore my joy.

Why am I discouraged? Why is my heart so sad? I will put my hope in God! I will praise him again—my Savior and my God! PSALM 42:11

DAY 267

A prayer about OPPOSITION

When my faith engenders hostility and antagonism

DEAR JESUS,

Today I was mocked for being your follower, and I was shocked at the hostility. As I was explaining my stance on a specific issue and how I came to that position because of what the Bible teaches, people whom I thought were friends attacked me verbally. Instead of respectfully talking about the topic and my beliefs, they laughed and made disparaging comments about your Word and Christians. You repeatedly told your disciples that they would face strong opposition, including mocking, slander, arrest, and physical harm. They experienced much more pain and suffering for their faith than I probably ever will, yet they faithfully endured and continued to tell others about you. And even now, my brothers and sisters in Christ in many places around the world are encountering extreme persecution. My immediate response to my "persecution" was surprise and hurt, but then I became angry. I know that's not your way. Please give me the strength to respond with love and grace. And please open my persecutors' eyes to the truth, to the gospel. They need to know you, too.

God blesses you when people mock you and persecute you and lie about you and say all sorts of evil things against you because you are my followers. Be happy about it! Be very glad! For a great reward awaits you in heaven. And remember, the ancient prophets were persecuted in the same way.

MATTHEW 5:11-12

A prayer about STANDING FIRM
When I am confronted and accused

PRECIOUS SAVIOR,
I recently encountered hostility—not totally unexpected, but certainly more intense than I had anticipated. I was wrongfully accused, and I'm pretty sure the animosity stems from my faith. The fact that I profess to be your follower, determined to live your way, is problematic for those with questionable morals and ethics. I remember that you told your early disciples to expect opposition. You told them not to "worry in advance about how to answer" but instead, to trust you fully. You also challenged them to stand firm. That's what I determine to do, Lord, with your help. I know what is right, and I will not give in. Regardless of the pressure, I will stand strong, my feet firmly planted on your Word, confident that you will give me "the right words and . . . wisdom." Whatever the final outcome, my faith—my relationship with you—is far more valuable than anything this world has to offer. So I commit the entire situation into your hand, dear Jesus. Give me strength and courage, words and wisdom.

Don't worry in advance about how to answer the charges against you, for I will give you the right words and such wisdom that none of your opponents will be able to reply or refute you! . . . And everyone will hate you because you are my followers. But not a hair of your head will perish! By standing firm, you will win your souls.
LUKE 21:14-15, 17-19

DAY 269

A prayer about STRENGTH
When I understand God's work for me and in me

ALMIGHTY GOD,

After you parted the Red Sea and brought your people through the waters safely, rescuing them from Pharaoh's army, the people praised you for your mighty work. They knew without a doubt that *you* alone had given them the victory. I have also seen miracles, not as dramatic as the one recorded in Exodus, but obvious displays of your strength. And I praise you for your divine intervention. Unfortunately, I tend to limit the exercise of your power to big events. In reality, daily I am the beneficiary of countless small, nearly invisible acts. I can do nothing without you. You provide opportunities, allow me to function physically, open and close doors, impart insight and ideas, craft my speech, and give me choices and the ability to choose wisely. Most important, you strengthen, encourage, and motivate me to resist temptation and do your will. Because of and through you alone, I can worship freely, serve selflessly, relate lovingly, and tell others of your glorious works. I submit to you, Lord. Open my eyes to see you more clearly.

The LORD is my strength and my song; he has given me victory. This is my God, and I will praise him—my father's God, and I will exalt him! EXODUS 15:2

DAY 270

A prayer about LOST AND FOUND
When I remember what God did for me

MY FATHER,

In Luke 15 Jesus tells three "lost and found" parables. In these stories, something valuable is lost: a helpless animal, an inanimate coin, and a rebellious boy. And on all three occasions, great rejoicing ensues when the lost has been found. I see myself in these situations, Lord. I certainly am dumb enough to wander off from safety. At times I feel just like the coin, seemingly out of sight and forgotten. But mostly I identify with the son, choosing to go my own way. I wandered far from your love and protection. You saw me in my lost condition and yearned to find me. I certainly didn't deserve or earn your favor, but you sought and saved me. And what really blows me away is the rejoicing part. I did nothing except turn, run to your arms, and accept your embrace. But heaven sings and throws a party! I was lost, but now I'm found—amazing grace!

If a man has a hundred sheep and one of them gets lost, what will he do? Won't he leave the ninety-nine others in the wilderness and go to search for the one that is lost until he finds it? And when he has found it, he will joyfully carry it home on his shoulders. When he arrives, he will call together his friends and neighbors, saying, "Rejoice with me because I have found my lost sheep." In the same way, there is more joy in heaven over one lost sinner who repents and returns to God than over ninety-nine others who are righteous and haven't strayed away! LUKE 15:4-7

DAY 271

A prayer about RIGHTEOUSNESS
When I consider my "good works"

MY SOVEREIGN,
I can get so full of myself, especially when I compare my works for the Kingdom to what others do. I begin to think I am doing well and that you should be proud of me, even implying that you are fortunate to have someone with my righteousness as your child. Forgive me, God, for my arrogance and pride. I need to constantly remember that I am a sinner saved by grace, that I was absolutely lost and without hope, and that my salvation rests on the finished work of Christ alone. All my "righteous deeds," my good works, are "but filthy rags"—worthless and useless, of no effect in my relationship with you. I know you want me to obey your commandments, to do your will, but all those works should happen as a *result* of our relationship as I respond to your love with my acts of love for you. I know you don't *need* me, but you have chosen me and continue to choose me to do your work in the world. Thank you!

We are all infected and impure with sin. When we display our righteous deeds, they are nothing but filthy rags. Like autumn leaves, we wither and fall, and our sins sweep us away like the wind. ISAIAH 64:6

DAY 272 *Prayerful Moment*

A prayer about DEPRESSION
When I'm feeling down

O LORD,
This was a rough day, and I feel bad about myself. My emotions are on edge, my eyes welling up. Life seems gloomy and threatening. I feel like David in the cave, when he was hiding from Saul. And as he did, I plead for your intervention. Give me your peace, I pray, and a good night's sleep. And help me awaken with renewed hope.

Come quickly, LORD, and answer me, for my depression deepens. Don't turn away from me, or I will die. Let me hear of your unfailing love each morning, for I am trusting you.
PSALM 143:7-8

DAY 273 *Prayerful Moment*

A prayer about WISDOM
When I want what is truly best

LORD,
You told King Solomon that he could ask you for anything, and you would give it to him. He asked for wisdom—a *wise* choice. I'm not a king, but I do influence others, and I want to do that well. And I definitely need to know right from wrong. So I, too, pray for understanding to know what to do and also for courage and strength to do it.

Give me an understanding heart so that I can govern your people well and know the difference between right and wrong.
1 KINGS 3:9

A prayer about WINNERS AND LOSERS
When I favor some people over others

SPIRIT OF GOD,
Society is enamored of celebrities. Rich and famous folks are featured in news stories, tabloids, and television shows. And wherever they go, they get special attention. That attitude, unfortunately, has invaded the church. We fawn over a well-to-do person (potential large donor), someone with influence (great connections), or a good-looking visitor while ignoring or even looking with disdain on the ragged visitor, the infirm senior, the mentally challenged adult, or the sullen middle schooler. That's how I sometimes act, and I am so sorry. The Bible says much about ministering to the poor, and Jesus invited children and society's outcasts to come to him. But often those people are invisible to me as I rush to greet the others who are more like me or whom I would like to meet. At those times, my motives certainly are not godly. When I lean that direction, Holy Spirit, convict me. Please open my eyes to *everyone* and help me love in Jesus' name.

My dear brothers and sisters, how can you claim to have faith in our glorious Lord Jesus Christ if you favor some people over others? . . . If you give special attention and a good seat to the rich person, but you say to the poor one, "You can stand over there, or else sit on the floor"—well, doesn't this discrimination show that your judgments are guided by evil motives? JAMES 2:1, 3-4

A prayer about ROUTINE
When I am simply going through the motions

SPIRIT OF GOD,
Blah. That's the best way to describe my spiritual life right now. I'm committed to following you, but I don't seem to be growing, and I'm not doing very well with the spiritual disciplines. I have daily devotions in the morning when I read from a book, but my mind wanders as I think about my to-do list. I pray, but mostly quick prayers or by habit, at meals and special occasions. I attend church regularly, but my worship seems superficial. In fact, I cannot remember when something in a service brought me to tears or I felt "blessed." I also can't recall when I last took time for silence, solitude, and meditation. My life has become ordinary, predictable. I'm thankful that I've established these routines, but I don't like the feeling that I am simply going through the motions in my relationship with you. Help me to break the routine, to create space, to feel more, and to go deeper. I want to learn from your Word, to experience your presence, to do great things for you.

You humble yourselves by going through the motions of penance, bowing your heads like reeds bending in the wind. You dress in burlap and cover yourselves with ashes. Is this what you call fasting? Do you really think this will please the LORD? ISAIAH 58:5

DAY 276

A prayer about BEING CHOSEN BY GOD
When I question my identity

LORD,
I remember, as a child, when teams were chosen on the playground. The "captains" would take turns pointing out whom they wanted. Everyone wanted to be on a strong team, of course, but the one thing dreaded most was being chosen last. That person felt totally unwanted, rejected. I know I have felt that way. And all my life people have been defining me: what I can and cannot do, who I am (child, student, young person, adult, employee), and what I am like (physically attractive or plain, achiever or underachiever, slim or overweight, tall or short, poor or rich). Add my race, sex, nationality, political affiliation, and church membership, and I see myself as a confusing blend of characteristics and qualities that often fall short of what and who I want to be. But then I remember that I am yours. I belong to you, chosen, bought, redeemed, and brought into your family. Regardless of the other voices describing me, I know that I am yours, and that is all that matters. Thank you, Lord.

You are not like that, for you are a chosen people. You are royal priests, a holy nation, God's very own possession. As a result, you can show others the goodness of God, for he called you out of the darkness into his wonderful light.
1 PETER 2:9

DAY 277

A prayer about SENSITIVITY TO OTHERS

When I am unaware of people's needs

GOD OF LOVE AND MERCY,

Although I truly desire to love others as you do, I can be oblivious to the needs of people near me. Sometimes when a person has a breakdown or even commits suicide, family members, friends, and neighbors will say, "The signs were there, but I just didn't see them." After the fact, the evidence seems obvious but not at the time. I can do the same; in fact, more than just warning signals, people themselves may be invisible to me. So I wonder about the signs and the individuals I may not be seeing. I want to see people—really see and hear them—to be alert to their needs. Help me read body language, understand what people are *not* saying, and sense their emotions. And after showing me the truth about them—so that I recognize their fear, sorrow, and pain—enable me to do something to help. Often they just need someone to understand and to listen; at other times the need is more tangible. Help me to act in love.

Suppose you see a brother or sister who has no food or clothing, and you say, "Good-bye and have a good day; stay warm and eat well"—but then you don't give that person any food or clothing. What good does that do? JAMES 2:15-16

DAY 278

A prayer about DEFENDING THE FAITH
When I need to speak up for Christ

FATHER,

During the day I often hear disparaging comments about Christianity, sometimes outright disbelief and blasphemy. I want to speak up, but I'm not sure what to say or how to say it. And when people use my Lord's name as a swear word or ridicule you or your people, I hurt inside and want to defend the truth. Yet I know that you need no defense from me. You are the sovereign and omnipotent God, and I'm just a tiny voice. At the same time, however, I know that you want believers to stand for the truth, to defend the faith entrusted to us. So I ask for courage, Lord, to say what I must. I also ask for words, Father, the cogent arguments that will cause others to reconsider their position and think about you. And I ask, most of all, for love—to see these people not as antagonists or as the enemy, but as lost souls who desperately need you.

Dear friends, I had been eagerly planning to write to you about the salvation we all share. But now I find that I must write about something else, urging you to defend the faith that God has entrusted once for all time to his holy people.
JUDE 1:3

DAY 279 *Prayerful Moment*

A prayer about JUDGING OTHERS
When I make assumptions about people's actions

ALMIGHTY GOD,

I am so quick to judge others, especially their motives. If I am late, I have a good reason (or so I think). But if someone else isn't on time, I assume the worst. I do the same with how people spend money, dress, or miss deadlines. Forgive me, Lord. Help me to think the best of people, and even when they slip or sin, to be quick to forgive.

Do not judge others, and you will not be judged. Do not condemn others, or it will all come back against you. Forgive others, and you will be forgiven. LUKE 6:37

DAY 280 *Prayerful Moment*

A prayer about CHANGE
When I sense hardness in my heart

FATHER GOD,

You gave a powerful promise, through your prophet Ezekiel, to change the hearts of your people. Even when we live our own way, you don't give up on us. You love us, transform us, and guide us home. Thank you, Lord, for not giving up on me. O Father, forgive me for having a divided and hard heart. Change me on the inside, conforming me to the image of your dear Son.

I will give them singleness of heart and put a new spirit within them. I will take away their stony, stubborn heart and give them a tender, responsive heart. EZEKIEL 11:19

DAY 281

A prayer about INFLUENCE
When I consider those who look up to me

HEAVENLY FATHER,

I have never considered myself to be a role model for anyone. I see myself as a regular, normal person trying to do my best in this world while honoring you. But after a mom thanked me for being a good example for her child, I began thinking about who might be watching me. When I was younger, I remember looking up to aunts, uncles, Sunday school teachers, coaches, choir directors, school teachers, and older kids. I almost idolized some. So I realize that I *do* influence people, especially the children I lead, by how I act and talk and by my opinions and ideas. So I pray that I will be a good example, a positive influence, on all who look up to me. But I also should consider who and what is affecting *me*. Many entities try to influence my financial decisions, voting choices, clothing, and hair styles—just about every aspect of life. More important, the culture tries to influence my values. I want my values aligned with yours, loving you with all my heart, soul, mind, and strength.

[The LORD said,] "If you speak good words rather than worthless ones, you will be my spokesman. You must influence them; do not let them influence you!"
JEREMIAH 15:19

DAY 282

A prayer about RESTORATION
When I am falling apart

MY LOVING FATHER AND LIFE BUILDER,
People who do housing restoration seek out and buy buildings that have fallen into disrepair. Then they fix them, restoring them to what they should be like, and then sell them for a profit. Right now I feel like a shabby home: neglected, torn, dusty, broken, and desperately needing repair. I confess that this has been my own doing—I have not worked at keeping my life in order by reading and applying your Word. Sin has been ripping the fabric of my life, and important relationships seem to be falling apart. I know you see value in me and can remake me into the kind of person you desire. I repent of my sins of commission and omission and humbly submit to you. Tear out and throw out what needs to go from every part of my life, your home. Remodel, add, and rebuild what you must. I acknowledge that the process will be painful, but necessary. Do with me as you will, restoring my hope, my joy, my life.

The high and lofty one who lives in eternity, the Holy One, says this: . . . "I restore the crushed spirit of the humble and revive the courage of those with repentant hearts."
ISAIAH 57:15

DAY 283

A prayer about THE WAY
When I need assurance of my salvation

MY GOD AND MY SALVATION,
I can identify with the questioning, doubting, and often stumbling disciples. One time when Jesus was trying to assure them of their destiny, they became confused and asked about "the way." I can hear Jesus answering them and speaking to me: "I am the way." Thank you, Lord, for providing the way for me to come to you. Jesus said "*the* way," not "*a* way," implying that there is only one way. Then to make sure everyone understood, he added, "No one can come to the Father except through me." Contemporary religion says many roads lead to the same destination, and that Jesus is just one of them. But I know better, Lord, because I know you. When Jesus left this earth, he went to prepare a place for all believers, for me. Someday soon I will go there to live with him forever. And I'm on my way, *the* way, there. Whenever I need assurance of my salvation, help me remember this incident, this story. I have Jesus, and he is all I need.

[Jesus said,] "When everything is ready, I will come and get you, so that you will always be with me where I am. And you know the way to where I am going." "No, we don't know, Lord," Thomas said. "We have no idea where you are going, so how can we know the way?" Jesus told him, "I am the way, the truth, and the life. No one can come to the Father except through me." JOHN 14:3-6

DAY 284

A prayer about ANXIETY
When I'm feeling worried

MY SAVIOR,
Normally I am not a worrier, but certain situations bring out the anxiety in me. And I felt it today as I moved through my responsibilities, the growing sense of dread that things were not going to work out. I know better, of course. I know that you love me and are guiding my steps, and because you are sovereign, in control, I should trust you fully. But when I'm in the middle of a difficult situation and begin to worry, that trust eludes me. I find in Philippians, however, the antidote: I should pray about everything—unloading my fearful thoughts, anxious emotions, and needs—thanking you all the while for what you have done and are doing in my life. I need *you*, Lord. Thank you for being with me and for me, all the time, in every situation.

Don't worry about anything; instead, pray about everything. Tell God what you need, and thank him for all he has done.
PHILIPPIANS 4:6

A prayer about FAITH
When I feel my trust slipping

LOVING FATHER,
I have been a Christ follower for many years, and I admit that I can take you and your work for granted. I was not always that way. Early in my relationship with you I was like a child—laughing, singing, playing, and taking Daddy's hand and walking confidently and unafraid. I exulted in my new life—free, forgiven, faith filled, and fearless. But since then, I have grown a bit calloused, allowing my brain to rule my heart, and losing joy in the process. Faith means believing the facts about you, that you sent Jesus to die for me. Faith means trusting you fully, knowing that you love me, want the best for me, and will never lead me the wrong way. And faith means taking action, committing every step to you. I want to be a child again, Lord, not in age but in wonder, trusting fully in you. Pull me into your lap. Bless me and build my faith. Help me lean wholly on you, knowing without question that you are good and that you are mine.

I trust in your unfailing love. I will rejoice because you have rescued me. PSALM 13:5

DAY 286 *Prayerful Moment*

A prayer about WILLINGNESS
When God calls

GOD,
When you asked who would be your messenger, Isaiah immediately responded, "Send me." He didn't know what you wanted him to do, but he knew you and that was enough. As I read your Word, I hear you challenging me to represent you. Help me not to delay or make excuses. I want to be like Isaiah. Whatever you want me to do, "Here I am. Send me."

I heard the Lord asking, "Whom should I send as a messenger to this people? Who will go for us?" I said, "Here I am. Send me." ISAIAH 6:8

DAY 287 *Prayerful Moment*

A prayer about CHARACTER
When I have to make tough choices

DEAR GOD,
I know a person's true character is revealed under pressure when no one is looking. My character was tested and tempted today. But I remembered I want to respond as Jesus would, so I made the right choices. Thank you for empowering me to think and act in ways that respect you.

May you always be filled with the fruit of your salvation—the righteous character produced in your life by Jesus Christ—for this will bring much glory and praise to God.
PHILIPPIANS 1:11

A prayer about DISTRACTIONS
When I look away from my goal

O LORD,

Ever since I first trusted Christ as my Savior, my goal in life has been to glorify you, to honor you with my thoughts, words, and deeds. But I can become distracted as my eyes are drawn elsewhere, like a child whose attention is captured by a new toy. Some days the distraction is a relationship issue; at other times, it's a conflict at work or in my career. Today, I was pulled aside by concerns over dwindling finances and insecurity about the future. I think of Peter when he took a few steps out of the boat onto the water and then began to sink when he took his eyes off Jesus. Today in the same way, the waves of worry began washing over me. I forgot your promises to be with me always, to care for me, and to uphold me. I looked at the problems and not at the Savior. Please help me, I pray, to "turn [my] eyes upon Jesus, look full in his wonderful face. And the things of earth will grow strangely dim, in the light of his glory and grace."

Look straight ahead, and fix your eyes on what lies before you. Mark out a straight path for your feet; stay on the safe path. Don't get sidetracked. PROVERBS 4:25-27

A prayer about LOVE FOR GOD
When my devotion seems weak

ALMIGHTY GOD,

I profess to love you, holding you at the top of my priorities, but then I make choices that belie those words and reveal me as a hypocrite. In Jesus' conversation with a lawyer, recorded in Luke, he affirmed that we are to love you with all of who we are—heart, soul, strength, and mind. So Father, right now I ask you to change my *heart*, my deepest desires, conforming them to your will. The word *soul* speaks to my character, what I am like on the inside. So please make me your kind of person. As for my *strength*, the manner in which I live, please empower me to speak and act in accordance with your will. And transform my *mind*, I pray. Keep me from those thoughts and ideas that would pull me away from you. I know these changes won't be easy and will involve a process of my continuing to submit to you every day. But I want to be your person, fully devoted to you—heart, soul, strength, and mind.

The man answered, "'You must love the LORD *your God with all your heart, all your soul, all your strength, and all your mind.' And, 'Love your neighbor as yourself.'" "Right!" Jesus told him. "Do this and you will live!"*

LUKE 10:27-28

A prayer about the BIBLE
When I read God's Word

HEAVENLY FATHER,

I read the Bible this morning, and your words stayed with me throughout the day, especially certain passages, informing my actions as I went about my daily routine. I study Scripture, not as a duty, but because I know that on those pages, in those words, you have revealed who you are and how you want your people to live. I am convinced that the Bible is my ultimate authority for faith and practice. As I read, I see you in action—creating, sustaining, loving, reaching, redeeming, forgiving, judging, and guiding. I hear you teaching, reprimanding, affirming, and encouraging. I feel your heart. I see you deal with real people in their struggles. And I see Jesus. As I delve into your story, I also see myself and my need for you. Thank you for working through writers centuries ago to pen the words you desired and for keeping them from error, giving us the inspired Word of God. Through your Spirit, illuminate those words and give me the courage and strength to put those life principles into practice.

I will study your commandments and reflect on your ways.
I will delight in your decrees and not forget your word.
PSALM 119:15-16

A prayer about NECESSITIES
When I think about what I really need

O LORD,
My life is cluttered. I seem to have accumulated lots of "stuff" through the years. What is most disconcerting is that I purchased most of the items with the idea, at the time, that I definitely *needed* them: gadgets, labor-saving appliances, electronic gizmos, fashionable clothes, tools, and much more. Now I think, *What a waste!* and *What do I do with all this?* I need a refresher course on *necessities*, determining what I really need instead of what I think I need and giving in to ads or bowing to fads. I believe this is a stewardship issue. It is also about values and focus. Help me resist the pull of my sinful desires and the tendency to feed my hunger for more. Help me to be wise in my choices and not waste my limited resources on trivial purchases and pursuits. On the other hand, I don't want to be a tightwad and become obsessed with saving a buck. So with the wisdom, please give me generosity. And in all of this, Lord, please show me the true necessities of life.

O God, I beg two favors from you; let me have them before I die. First, help me never to tell a lie. Second, give me neither poverty nor riches! Give me just enough to satisfy my needs. For if I grow rich, I may deny you and say, "Who is the LORD?" And if I am too poor, I may steal and thus insult God's holy name. PROVERBS 30:7-9

A prayer about the IMAGE OF GOD
When I wonder how I am like my Creator

BLESSED CREATOR,

I hear much about the environment and taking care of the earth. I'm all for that. I also hear about not being cruel to animals and endangered species, and I agree with many of those positions, too. But I know that human beings stand at the pinnacle of your creation. After creating the world and all the other living creatures, in a special act you made the first man and woman in your image. Then you gave them responsibility and authority to care for everything else. People are special, unique—not just more-advanced animals. Theologians debate what being created in your image means—having a spiritual nature, moral sensitivity, ability to reason and speak, capacity for making free choices, the ability to be artistic, or something else? Whatever the answer, we are different, unique, and valued. Thank you, Lord, for creating *me* in your image and for the awesome privilege of knowing you and communicating with you. Help me remember that *all* other people, everywhere, are also your special creations and I should treat them with respect and value life.

If anyone takes a human life, that person's life will also be taken by human hands. For God made human beings in his own image. GENESIS 9:6

DAY 293 *Prayerful Moment*

A prayer about COMMITMENT
When I become wishy-washy in my faith

LORD OF HEAVEN AND EARTH,
You are sovereign, and you love me. At times, though, I feel the pull of the world's values and forget my promise to love you with all my heart, soul, mind, and strength. I want to serve you and be fully committed to you and your mission. Please help me focus my mind on you, and give me the will and the strength to choose your way.

As we live in God, our love grows more perfect.
1 JOHN 4:17

DAY 294 *Prayerful Moment*

A prayer about QUIET
When my life becomes noisy

JESUS,
Often in your earthly ministry you retreated from the noisy crowds to a place of solitude and silence. If you needed quiet time alone to commune with your Father, how much more do I need to spend time with you! Please show me how to rework my schedule to regularly spend time with you, away from the noise and clutter. Then help me to share my deepest thoughts, and listen.

After sending [the disciples] home, [Jesus] went up into the hills by himself to pray. Night fell while he was there alone.
MATTHEW 14:23

A prayer about STEWARDSHIP
When I need to know how to invest God's gifts

LORD ABOVE,

You own everything and have allowed me to use earth's bountiful resources. Along with this privilege, you have given your human creations the responsibility to care for them. You have also entrusted personal resources for me to steward: time, talent, and treasure. I know these gifts are valuable and limited and should not be squandered. Instead, you want me to invest them for the Kingdom. My time on earth is limited, so I pray that I will use my remaining days and years to serve you well, reaching out to others, spreading the Good News, and spending quality time with you. I don't want to waste or bury these resources. You have also endowed me with unique talents and abilities. These, too, should be used for your glory. Please keep me from laziness or taking these gifts for granted. Help me develop and exercise them to honor you. And you have allowed me to have money and possessions. Show me how to invest them to further your work and give me the courage to do so. I take stewardship seriously.

The master said, "Well done, my good and faithful servant. You have been faithful in handling this small amount, so now I will give you many more responsibilities. Let's celebrate together!" MATTHEW 25:23

DAY 296

A prayer about POWER FOR LIVING
When I face the challenges of each day

HOLY SPIRIT,

You have made dramatic changes in me—my outlook on life, how I relate to people, my motives, my goals, my values and priorities . . . every area. I am not the person I was. Thank you. This gives me hope for the future because I know you are constantly working in me, changing my desires and making me more like Christ. I am a new person inside, and I want to live for Christ every day and in every situation. I tend to be self-reliant so I often try to live the Christian life through hard work and determination, but that approach just ends in frustration and disappointment. That's because I'm doing it all in my own strength. What a futile exercise! Instead, I need to depend totally on you and your power working through me. I know that I am supposed to love my enemies, resist temptation, give godly counsel, stand for truth, serve others selflessly, steward my resources wisely, and more—all only possible by God's grace and through his strength. Holy Spirit, please empower me.

May [God] give you the power to accomplish all the good things your faith prompts you to do. Then the name of our Lord Jesus will be honored because of the way you live, and you will be honored along with him. This is all made possible because of the grace of our God and Lord, Jesus Christ. 2 THESSALONIANS 1:11-12

A prayer about TRUSTWORTHINESS
When I wonder if others can put their confidence in me

ALMIGHTY GOD,

As one who represents you, I want to be the kind of person who reflects your nature. Daniel was a captive in a foreign land—far from home, family, friends, and familiar surroundings. He could have been angry and bitter or devious and disingenuous. But the opposite occurred; the pressures of that environment revealed his true character. Although they tried hard, those who opposed him in the government could find nothing wrong with Daniel's work. In fact, "he was faithful, always responsible, and completely trustworthy." Quite a positive description and reputation—and representing you, what an amazing impact he had on the nation. At times I, too, feel as though I am an alien in the land because of my values and morals. People can be put off by my declaration of allegiance to you, Lord God, and even look for ways to criticize or condemn me. I pray that, like Daniel, my character will shine through and bring glory to you. I pray that everyone, even my opponents, will know that they can put their confidence in me.

The other administrators and high officers began searching for some fault in the way Daniel was handling government affairs, but they couldn't find anything to criticize or condemn. He was faithful, always responsible, and completely trustworthy. DANIEL 6:4

DAY 298

A prayer about a THORN IN THE FLESH
When I need to be humbled

GRACIOUS GOD,
I found myself becoming quite full of myself today, and I'm ashamed. Basking in accomplishment and adulation, I puffed with pride. I think that in Jesus' day I would have been a good candidate to be a Pharisee. I remember the apostle Paul, reflecting on an amazing spiritual experience, saying that you had given him a "thorn" to keep him from being proud of what he had seen and heard. Whether physical, emotional, or whatever, this struggle, the thorn, was a painful, daily reminder that he was nothing in himself and totally dependent on you. Paul wanted his attitude, values, lifestyle, and actions to point only to Christ and his work in him. I certainly do not wish or ask for a thorny problem, but what I desire *more* is to be your kind of person in this world, serving you with grace and humility. Please purge from me this tendency toward self-aggrandizement, always looking to promote my image and to get the credit. If that means giving me a "thorn in my flesh," then so be it. I am your humble servant.

If I wanted to boast, I would be no fool in doing so, because I would be telling the truth. But I won't do it, because I don't want anyone to give me credit beyond what they can see in my life or hear in my message, even though I have received such wonderful revelations from God. So to keep me from becoming proud, I was given a thorn in my flesh, a messenger from Satan to torment me and keep me from becoming proud. 2 CORINTHIANS 12:6-7

DAY 299

A prayer about ANGER
When my feelings seem out of control

DEAR LORD,
I blew it today. I lost my temper, and not to just anyone, but someone I care about. I want to rationalize—I was having a bad day, the traffic gridlock got to me, I didn't have a good night's sleep, I needed my coffee, and what I said was technically true—but if I'm honest, I have no excuse. I was out of control and wrong, and I used a hateful tone and made cutting comments. I know I need to ask forgiveness of my friend, but I need to lay it out before you first. Please help me, Father, to think before I speak, to consider the effects of my attitude and words, and to "bless" others rather than "curse" them. Please fill me with your Spirit and take control. I want to be known as a positive, joyful person who sees and affirms the good in others. I want to be more like Christ.

"Don't sin by letting anger control you." Don't let the sun go down while you are still angry, for anger gives a foothold to the devil. EPHESIANS 4:26-27

DAY 300 *Prayerful Moment*

A prayer about SEEING NEEDS
When I need to look through the Savior's eyes

JESUS,

Surrounded by multitudes, you reached out to individuals. Whatever the label—Pharisee, fisherman, leper, prostitute—you saw the person, someone who was hurting and needing you. I can easily dismiss whole groups of people, but you touched them all. Give me your vision, Savior. Help me see people's real needs and serve them with your selfless love.

The King will say, "I tell you the truth, when you [helped] one of the least of these my brothers and sisters, you were doing it to me!" MATTHEW 25:40

DAY 301 *Prayerful Moment*

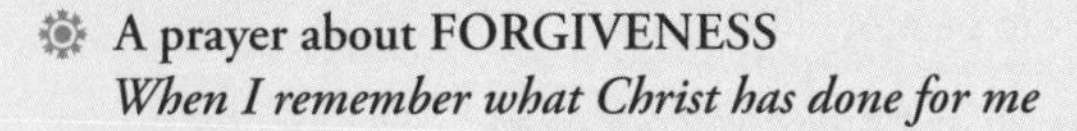

A prayer about FORGIVENESS
When I remember what Christ has done for me

MY FATHER,

I am totally forgiven—washed clean, declared "not guilty," set free! No metaphor can fully capture what you did for me—and all because of Jesus and by your mercy and grace. I was guilty, Lord, and deserved only judgment and punishment. But you saved me! Thank you.

Oh, what joy for those whose disobedience is forgiven, whose sin is put out of sight! Yes, what joy for those whose record the LORD *has cleared of guilt, whose lives are lived in complete honesty!* PSALM 32:1-2

DAY 302

A prayer about COMPLACENCY
When I take God for granted

FATHER GOD,
I don't know how it happens. Maybe I just get too busy and consumed with my own affairs, but I easily take you, your goodness, and your blessings for granted. It seems to be a fallback position, and I act as though I have forgotten your mighty works, profound love, and continuing grace for me. Every day I need to remember that I am a sinner and that Jesus died for me, in my place, on the cross. I desperately need you, Lord. When I become complacent in my faith, I tend to become self-focused and overlook my mistakes and transgressions. Instead, I want to be a person who takes sin seriously and lives fully, rejoicing in my salvation. I also don't want to be complacent about the fate of those who don't know you. Infuse me with urgency, realizing that you give me many opportunities to tell others about Christ. Thank you, Lord, for who you are, all you have done through Jesus, what you are doing in me by the Spirit, and the future you have planned.

I will search with lanterns in Jerusalem's darkest corners to punish those who sit complacent in their sins. They think the LORD will do nothing to them, either good or bad.
ZEPHANIAH 1:12

A prayer about OVERCOMING
When I feel pressed and oppressed

LORD IN HEAVEN,
"Faith is the victory that overcomes the world"—so goes the old song based on this passage in 1 John. I need to remember the truth of those words these days because the world seems to be closing in. Daily I battle against worldly values, ideas, pressures, and temptations. But you have promised that "every child of God defeats this evil world." Our victory comes through faith. I claim that promise, Lord. I believe that Jesus is the Son of God and that by trusting in him I have been forgiven and made completely new. Your Spirit lives in me, empowering me to resist Satan and to do what pleases you. I also know that you are all powerful—nothing can stand against you—and your mighty power is available to me. I know I cannot do this on my own. So right now I ask you to strengthen me to stand up to all that the world throws at me. I want to be an overcomer.

Every child of God defeats this evil world, and we achieve this victory through our faith. And who can win this battle against the world? Only those who believe that Jesus is the Son of God. 1 JOHN 5:4-5

DAY 304

A prayer about COMPLAINING
When I tend to whine

HEAVENLY FATHER,
Maybe I didn't get enough sleep last night, with what was on my mind and all that tossing and turning, or had a bad breakfast or hated the weather or the traffic or . . . , but in any case, I was in a sour mood today. I felt tired, had a headache, and seemed sensitive to *everything*. My disposition and conversations were negative, and I seemed to find fault in every situation with every person—no big blowups, but snarling and bickering all day. When someone made a statement, even about something as innocuous as a favorite TV show, my first response was to disagree. I don't like that version of me, Father, and I'm sure no one else does either. I certainly do not appreciate other people acting that way, so why should I be an exception? I know the world does not revolve around my schedule and needs, but sometimes I forget that. Lord, instead of being a complainer, I want to be known as an encourager. Please change my outlook and attitude and help me shine for you—every day.

Do everything without complaining and arguing, so that no one can criticize you. Live clean, innocent lives as children of God, shining like bright lights in a world full of crooked and perverse people. PHILIPPIANS 2:14-15

DAY 305

A prayer about FUN

When I begin to think too seriously about myself and life

DEAR LORD,

Everything seems to be a big deal these days and oh so serious—major decisions, relationship drama, national politics, international crises, and many other concerns and worries—and life has taken on a gray, somber hue. Today I passed an elementary school playground with children at recess. They were swinging, playing, laughing, and running, just enjoying the weather and chasing each other around. And I remembered how I used to be just like those kids, finding humor in most situations, goofing off and laughing with friends, and having fun. When did life get so grim? I want to exult in your love, to rejoice in your presence, and dance. I know you have a sense of humor; after all, you created the platypus . . . and me. Yes, theology is deep, and we dare not take your Word lightly; serious problems need serious solutions. But you have said that I should be happy in you and that you expect rejoicing. Please open my eyes to your joyful work; help me lighten up!

Happy are those who hear the joyful call to worship, for they will walk in the light of your presence, LORD. They rejoice all day long in your wonderful reputation. They exult in your righteousness. PSALM 89:15-16

A prayer about WOUNDS
When I am deeply hurt

HEAVENLY FATHER,

You know everything I am going through—all the time. You know when I have been hurt, grievously wounded, and you feel with me. I know that many of my wounds have been self-inflicted, results of my mistakes and sins. Thank you for forgiving me and getting me back on my feet. At other times, I have felt wounded by a friend who has spoken truth to me, painful words that I needed to hear. Thank you for giving me those relationships—people who care enough to confront and correct me. You have used them mightily in my life. Recently I have struggled physically because I am a frail and weak human being, subject to accidents, infections, and other maladies in this fallen world. And you have been with me, giving me your peace and guiding the physicians. I have also been wounded by the sins of others, but you have stood with me and have given me strength to endure. In each wounding, I remember the wounds Jesus bore for me, a lost, undeserving sinner. I praise you.

[The Lord] heals the brokenhearted and bandages their wounds. PSALM 147:3

DAY 307 *Prayerful Moment*

A prayer about CHEATING
When I am tempted to take moral and ethical shortcuts

GOD,

In ancient Israel, some merchants used dishonest scales to cheat customers. That's not my style. But I'm often tempted to cut corners at work, with finances, or in relationships. It is usually the easy way, and I can quickly rationalize it. Besides the fact that it's wrong, I know that cheating in small matters can escalate and become a way of life. I'm *not* a cheater, Lord. Help me always to be honest.

Honesty guides good people; dishonesty destroys treacherous people. . . . The godly are directed by honesty; the wicked fall beneath their load of sin. PROVERBS 11:3, 5

DAY 308 *Prayerful Moment*

A prayer about FAILURE
When I suffer a major setback

GOD,

Today not only didn't I win, but I failed . . . miserably. I disappointed myself; even worse, I let down people who were counting on me. I feel like a total failure. I know you don't see me that way and you love me for who I am, not for my accomplishments. But I'm struggling, Father. Comfort me, and show me the next step to take.

My health may fail, and my spirit may grow weak, but God remains the strength of my heart; he is mine forever.
PSALM 73:26

A prayer about IRRITATIONS

When I become increasingly annoyed by people and situations

GOD,

Life seems to be filled with irritations lately. Certain people have irksome mannerisms that get under my skin. I seem to be meeting irritations at every turn: drivers who go too slow or too fast or think they can cut me off because they put on a turn signal or don't use turn signals at all; clerks or waitstaff who act indifferent or rude or who get the order wrong; people who are late or early, who tell the same joke or story repeatedly, or who talk too loud or too soft or too much or too little; and all those little annoyances such as things that break, don't work correctly, have strange directions, are too big or too small or too hot or too cold. At times I want to run away because these people and things get to me. Wait—maybe the problem is me, Lord. Please help me take my eyes off myself and my needs and change me from picky to pleasant and from negative to positive . . . and to stop being so irritating myself.

Search me, O God, and know my heart; test me and know my anxious thoughts. Point out anything in me that offends you, and lead me along the path of everlasting life.

PSALM 139:23-24

A prayer about SALT AND LIGHT
When I analyze my personal impact on the world

DEAR JESUS,
You told your disciples and the gathered crowd that your followers should be salt and light in the world. Salt is a preservative, and I know that believers have served this purpose, helping to preserve society, restraining evil and promoting good. But then and now, salt also adds flavor—and thirst. So I wonder how flavorful I am. Are people better because of their association with me? Do I add hope, joy, and love to life? And are people thirsty for you and your Word because they know me? I want to be useful for you, Lord; I want to be salty salt! You also used light as a metaphor. Light illuminates, highlights, and gives direction, all qualities that should describe me. My "light" should shine through my words and actions. People should praise you because of what they see in me. May it be so. I also want to illuminate the truth of your Word, to put the spotlight on you, and to guide sinners home. O Savior, help me be your light.

You are the salt of the earth. But what good is salt if it has lost its flavor? Can you make it salty again? It will be thrown out and trampled underfoot as worthless. You are the light of the world—like a city on a hilltop that cannot be hidden. No one lights a lamp and then puts it under a basket. Instead, a lamp is placed on a stand, where it gives light to everyone in the house. In the same way, let your good deeds shine out for all to see, so that everyone will praise your heavenly Father. MATTHEW 5:13-16

A prayer about LIFE LESSONS
When I need to "go to school"

MY TEACHER,

Every day you present me with many opportunities to learn and grow. For quite a while my prayers have included requests for every fruit of the Spirit: love, joy, peace, patience, kindness, goodness, faithfulness, gentleness, and self-control. Certainly these are by-products of the Spirit's work in my life, but they need to be learned and used. And you have answered my prayers and have given me those situations. When someone pushes my emotional buttons and feelings of frustration and anger well up, I need to exercise gentleness and self-control. In situations where waiting is necessary, I need to exercise patience. In times of stress, I need peace. And so on. You have also provided lessons on stewardship and generosity, being a good friend, serving selflessly, being humble, and courageously speaking up for the gospel. I have also had to learn many lessons the hard way, asking for and giving forgiveness. I want to continue to grow in my faith, to be a student of your Word and learn from you. So I ask for more faith-stretching occasions. Teach me, Lord.

[Jesus said,] "Take my yoke upon you. Let me teach you, because I am humble and gentle at heart, and you will find rest for your souls. For my yoke is easy to bear, and the burden I give you is light." MATTHEW 11:29-30

DAY 312

A prayer about GRATITUDE
When my outlook needs adjusting

SAVIOR,

I'm not usually a negative person, but these days being positive is difficult, considering all the world's problems and my personal challenges. I confess that I have been looking inward on my struggles and outward on the fallen and broken planet. I have almost a daily "Woe is me" pity party. Instead, I need to look *upward*, to you, remembering your promises and all that you have given and are giving to me. When I do that, my whole outlook changes, and I am overwhelmed with feelings of gratitude for who you are and for what you have done. Thank you, Lord! Paul told the Thessalonian believers (and me) to "be thankful in all circumstances." For a while I thought I had to praise and thank you *for* everything that happened to, in, and around me, including pain, sorrow, sinful acts, and terrible tragedies. That could happen only if I faked thankfulness. Instead, you want us to thank you *in* everything we face, grateful for who you are and for your perfect plans. Please keep me looking up.

Be thankful in all circumstances, for this is God's will for you who belong to Christ Jesus. 1 THESSALONIANS 5:18

DAY 313

A prayer about WONDER

When I need to see life as a child does

MY FATHER,

I love working with children, watching them discover and learn. They throw themselves into each activity with gusto and say whatever is on their minds. But the best treat is seeing their expressions of joy at a new truth or experience. I have grown and matured, and that's good, but in the process I seem to have lost that sense of wonder and amazement. Very little affects me that way. Even the word *wonderful* has lost its meaning. Yet I am immersed in marvel, surrounded by miracles, from microscopic organisms to stellar constellations and human beings with eternal souls. Open my eyes, Lord; open my heart. You are doing something in my own day, in my own *life*. The fact that I can have this conversation with you is amazing. You also provide, protect, guide, and convict as your Spirit shapes me into the kind of person you want me to be. And right now this process is happening in countless thousands of lives of every nation and race, each one important to you. I am in awe.

The LORD replied, "Look around at the nations; look and be amazed! For I am doing something in your own day, something you wouldn't believe even if someone told you about it." HABAKKUK 1:5

DAY 314 *Prayerful Moment*

A prayer about WORSHIP
When I walk into church

LORD,
When at church services, I usually enjoy the singing, preaching, sacraments, and interactions with others. I think I'm in a worship rut, however, with my mind wandering. Please refresh my soul. I want to again worship you in "truth"—understanding your Word—and "spirit"—fully engaged as I enter your holy presence.

True worshipers will worship the Father in spirit and in truth. The Father is looking for those who will worship him that way. JOHN 4:23

DAY 315 *Prayerful Moment*

A prayer about SINCERITY
When I am tempted to fake it

FATHER,
I am repelled by insincerity—slick salespeople, shallow teachers, and phonies. I want people to speak the truth and to honestly express their thoughts and feelings. Yet today I found myself acting to make a positive impression. I want to be sincere in my actions and speech, meaning what I say. Only then will people believe what I say about you.

[Paul said,] "You see, we are not like the many hucksters who preach for personal profit. We preach the word of God with sincerity and with Christ's authority, knowing that God is watching us." 2 CORINTHIANS 2:17

A prayer about RESOLUTIONS
When I determine to improve

HEAVENLY FATHER,

Resolutions are easy to make and easy to break. Many people make them on January 1 because they want to change their lives, and the turning of the calendar, they hope, will mean a turn in their lives, a fresh start. I want to improve, especially in my relationship with you, but I don't want to overpromise and underdeliver. I know I cannot change on my own, so I am trusting you to change my desires and give me strength. Having said that, I make these promises to you:

- I will talk to you more, all through the day and at appointed times to go deeper and to listen.
- I will read the Bible daily, devotionally, and study it regularly. I will look for ways to apply your timeless truths to my life today.
- I will pray for my relatives, friends, coworkers, and neighbors who don't know you, and I ask for opportunities to share your Good News with them.
- I will look for ways to use my spiritual gifts.
- I will worship you with my whole being.

Amen.

It is not by force nor by strength, but by my Spirit, says the LORD of Heaven's Armies. ZECHARIAH 4:6

DAY 317

A prayer about BEING THE BEST

When I'm tempted to settle for "good" or "better"

LOVING GOD,

I had a good day today. I think I did relatively good work, lived well, and accomplished quite a bit. And I usually try to do even better. To be honest, however, I have to admit that my understanding of "good" and "better" comes from comparing myself with others. I have a good life compared to those who struggle, and I do good things compared to those who don't. I think I'm a good person. I also can use that standard to measure my performance, thinking that I'm doing well simply because my work is above average. I am good, and that should be enough. But I want to be the best, not for my sake, but to glorify you. I want to be *your* person, living up to *your* standards, regardless of how that compares to anyone else. I want to be more like Jesus. Help me be the best I can be for your sake. I want to hold nothing back and offer you my *best*—in how I work, relate to others, serve at church, and live.

You should earnestly desire the most helpful gifts. But now let me show you a way of life that is best of all.

1 CORINTHIANS 12:31

DAY 318

A prayer about STRESS
When life bears down on me

MY LORD AND SAVIOR,
Today was stressful, mostly because of obligations and deadlines. Metals are stressed to make them resistant to fractures, and athletes stress their muscles to make them stronger. Too much stress, however, can cause *dis*tress and breakdowns. I pray that what I am experiencing these days will strengthen me, so I can become more productive for you. But to be honest, I may be feeling a few small fractures developing. My mind is reeling, and my gut is clenching. The psalmists responded to stress by reading your Word and finding joy. I need to do the same. You told your disciples to expect trials but to take heart because you had overcome the world. That's a promise I can cling to. You are greater; through you I can overcome whatever I am experiencing. So now as I finish this day, please relieve my anxiety, erase my fears, remove the stress, and help me sleep in peace. When I arise tomorrow morning, give me joy and determination to meet the challenges of a new day.

[Jesus said,] "You may have peace in me. Here on earth you will have many trials and sorrows. But take heart, because I have overcome the world." JOHN 16:33

DAY 319

A prayer about the BREVITY OF LIFE
When I feel time slipping away

ETERNAL FATHER,

As I get older, the days, weeks, and years seem to fly with increasing speed. Sometimes I have to do the math to remember how old I am. And when I think of events of a decade or two ago, I feel as though they happened just yesterday. I don't want to yearn for or live in the past or fear the future, but I feel as though my life is slipping away much too quickly. The years seem to be growing increasingly shorter. Thank you, Lord, that you have more planned for me than my few years on earth. I know that life is short no matter how long I live, but eternity with you is forever. Help me, Father, to grow in wisdom so that I make the most of the time you give me, using my God-given talents and abilities for your glory, valuing others, taking advantage of the opportunities you provide, and rejoicing in the gift of each new day.

LORD, remind me how brief my time on earth will be. Remind me that my days are numbered—how fleeting my life is. You have made my life no longer than the width of my hand. My entire lifetime is just a moment to you; at best, each of us is but a breath. PSALM 39:4-5

DAY 320

A prayer about TEAMWORK
When I understand my role in the church

HEAVENLY FATHER,
I know teamwork is vital in sports, music, and other areas of life. Each member has a specific task to fulfill for the team, squad, choir, orchestra, partnership, task force, or committee for it to be successful. So why do I forget that important truth in the church? At times I act alone, without working with anyone else. Sometimes I am almost envious of others—their gifts and appointed roles. But I remember that the earthly collection of believers not only represents Christ but also, through the indwelling of the Holy Spirit, is his body. Paul explains how each member of the body has a special role to play and that all the parts must work together. I may have an upfront, public display of my gifts or another leadership role. But I may be called to a less obvious responsibility. Whatever the case, I must do my best, working together with other team members, for your glory. An orchestra has a concertmaster but also a "last chair"—both must play well. Wherever I am placed, I want to give my best.

[Christ] makes the whole body fit together perfectly. As each part does its own special work, it helps the other parts grow, so that the whole body is healthy and growing and full of love. EPHESIANS 4:16

DAY 321 *Prayerful Moment*

A prayer about CRITICISM
When I am the victim of unjust critical comments

GRACIOUS GOD,
The words cut deeply. Someone said my work was substandard, certainly not what it should be. I try to be open to criticism—I'll always have room for improvement—but this just was not true. The evaluation was nitpicky and small. I don't know the motive behind the accusation—whether innocent or malicious—but help me respond as Jesus would. May I act in love.

Malicious witnesses testify against me. They accuse me of crimes I know nothing about. PSALM 35:11

DAY 322 *Prayerful Moment*

A prayer about CONSCIENCE
When I sense an inner voice giving me direction

SPIRIT OF GOD,
Thank you for that inside voice that points me in the direction of doing what is right and avoiding what is wrong. And thank you, Spirit, for sensitizing me to sin. When I am tempted to do what I know is wrong, Lord, give me the strength to respond in a way that honors you. Please help me chose the right path and keep my conscience clear.

Cling to your faith in Christ, and keep your conscience clear. For some people have deliberately violated their consciences; as a result, their faith has been shipwrecked.
1 TIMOTHY 1:19

DAY 323

A prayer about VICTORY
When I'm in the heat of the battle

ALMIGHTY GOD,
I am in a battle, that's for sure. My day was packed with skirmishes, most unexpected. I understand from your Word that Satan and his minions are combating you and your people, so I should not be surprised by the attacks. Because these are spiritual forces, however, I shouldn't rely on my cunning and might. As the nation of Israel was preparing for war on their journey to the land you promised, you pledged to be with them and to give them the victory. And you did—often against seemingly insurmountable odds. My enemy is unseen but just as real. But having you with me and fighting for me assures his defeat. What a mighty Savior I serve! You have enlisted and equipped me. As your soldier, I submit to your leadership. As a *mere* soldier, I rely on your wisdom and strength. Tell me where to go and what to say and do, and I will obey. I can move forward with confidence, even into enemy territory, certain that together we will be victorious. Thank you, Lord.

Do not be afraid as you go out to fight your enemies today! Do not lose heart or panic or tremble before them. For the LORD *your God is going with you! He will fight for you against your enemies, and he will give you victory!*
DEUTERONOMY 20:3-4

DAY 324

A prayer about THE NARROW WAY
When I see so many going down the wrong road

HEAVENLY FATHER,

Jesus' statement about being the only way to you doesn't sit well with most people these days. Conventional wisdom says everyone is supposed to be open-minded and inclusive. We are told that many roads lead to God. So when someone dies, unless the person was notoriously evil, pundits, even religious leaders, say that he or she is in heaven. What a terrible deception . . . and so sad because most people believe these lies. Truth is always narrow, and being sincerely wrong is still wrong. I know many who are headed down the broad "highway to hell." That way is appealing with many allurements and virtually no restrictions, but it leads to destruction. My heart breaks for these people, Lord. Some days I feel as though I should grab a bullhorn and announce the truth or wear a placard and walk the streets, but I know neither would be very effective. Your way is narrow, but it is right—and it leads to life. Please give me opportunities and the words to point people lovingly to you.

You can enter God's Kingdom only through the narrow gate. The highway to hell is broad, and its gate is wide for the many who choose that way. But the gateway to life is very narrow and the road is difficult, and only a few ever find it.
MATTHEW 7:13-14

A prayer about PAYING IT FORWARD
When I am proactive in service

DEAR LORD,
Recently I have heard talk about "paying it forward." That is, instead of simply responding in kind to something done for us (returning the favor), we do a good deed for a stranger, who will then, hopefully, be motivated to do something good for someone else, and so forth. I shouldn't have to be reminded to act like this, because your Word tells believers to treat others the way we would like to be treated and to give our gifts in private, anonymously. My problem is that I usually want to be reciprocated for my gift—returned favor, strengthened relationship, public acknowledgment, heartfelt word of thanks. But loving other people your way means acting in their best interests with no strings attached. I want to do at least one random act of kindness every day—to see a need and meet it—and receive no credit or acknowledgment. Opportunities arise continually with a wide variety of people, so please make me aware of them. Then give me creative ideas for how to act and the courage to follow through.

When you give to someone in need, don't let your left hand know what your right hand is doing. Give your gifts in private, and your Father, who sees everything, will reward you. MATTHEW 6:3-4

DAY 326

A prayer about SEPARATION

When I wonder about what differentiates me from the world

PRECIOUS SAVIOR,

Many who profess to be your followers easily blend into the culture, with their values and priorities indistinguishable from people around them. Even their morals and ethics—including stances on honesty, marriage, health, and social issues—are similar. But your Word makes clear in both Testaments that believers should be different, that we should "separate" ourselves and stand out. I used to think, mistakenly, that separation from the world simply meant not doing certain activities. I know now, Lord, that while my behavior might change, the crucial differences are much deeper. Christians should be known for loving you with all their hearts, minds, and strength, and loving people, too. Love is the key—you told your disciples in the Upper Room that they would be marked as yours by their love for one another. O Lord, don't let me take the easy way and settle for fitting in, for all intents and purposes denying my relationship with you by not standing out. I want to be known as different, as someone with God-honoring values and standards, all the while pointing people to you.

Come out from among unbelievers, and separate yourselves from them, says the LORD. *Don't touch their filthy things, and I will welcome you.* 2 CORINTHIANS 6:17

A prayer about FACING "GIANTS"
When I encounter intimidating opposition

MY ALL-POWERFUL LORD,
At first no one took David seriously when he offered to confront Goliath. David showed no fear because of his total trust in you. Although just a boy, the youngest in the family, a shepherd, and with no battlefield experience, he ran to meet the challenge. David remembered your work in his life in the past and was confident that you were with him in the present. The negative odds were tremendous. On paper, no way could David win the battle. But he did. I need that kind of faith and courage, Lord. My "giants" are not heavily armed and armored, nine-foot warriors, but they loom large—strong, intimidating, and dangerous nonetheless: health concerns, financial challenges, career barriers and setbacks, looming decisions, interpersonal issues, and more. Every day I seem to encounter a new giant facing me across the valley. I need the courage and resourcefulness of David. Most important, I need you to stand with me and go before me, my strength and my salvation. Help me run to the battle—the victory belongs to you.

"The LORD who rescued me from the claws of the lion and the bear will rescue me from this Philistine!" Saul finally consented. "All right, go ahead," he said. "And may the LORD be with you!" 1 SAMUEL 17:37

DAY 328 *Prayerful Moment*

A prayer about PROSPERITY
When I consider real riches

DEAR JESUS,

I enjoy being comfortable and having sufficient financial resources. But if I need to experience abject poverty in the world's eyes to enjoy your riches, then may it be so. Sometimes I daydream about becoming wealthy, but that's a trap and a temptation I must resist. You left heaven's glory and became poor . . . for me. Thank you, Jesus.

You know the generous grace of our Lord Jesus Christ. Though he was rich, yet for your sakes he became poor, so that by his poverty he could make you rich. 2 CORINTHIANS 8:9

DAY 329 *Prayerful Moment*

A prayer about REMEMBRANCE
When I consider the Cross

SAVIOR,

I do think about you, your broken body and shed blood, each time I take the bread and wine of Communion. But I also need to remember your sacrifice in my daily life: relationships, work, struggles, and joys. Because of the Cross, my sins are forgiven. Because of you, I have hope and eternal life. Praise your name!

He took some bread and gave thanks to God for it. Then he broke it in pieces and gave it to the disciples, saying, "This is my body, which is given for you. Do this to remember me." LUKE 22:19

A prayer about SPIRITUAL FOOD
When I need nourishment

HEAVENLY FATHER,

I'm famished, spiritually. I need to be fed. As a new believer, I eagerly devoured the Word; I couldn't seem to get enough. Then I went through a period of feast or famine, times of intense interaction with you and your people and then long stretches of almost nothing. Just as you provided bread and meat for the people of Israel as they traveled to the Promised Land, you also give me opportunities to consume spiritual food daily. I shouldn't think I can store up provision for the next week, month, or year. Instead I need to partake now, when it is provided. Spiritual nourishment comes from reading and studying your Word, sitting under solid Bible teaching and preaching, engaging in corporate worship, spending time alone with you in prayer, and as Jesus said, doing your will. I dare not neglect any of these "meals." Please give me the discipline to consistently read the Scriptures, pray, and regularly attend church services. Lead me to individuals and a small group for community and care. And show me how I can serve.

Jesus replied, "I have a kind of food you know nothing about." "Did someone bring him food while we were gone?" the disciples asked each other. Then Jesus explained: "My nourishment comes from doing the will of God, who sent me, and from finishing his work." JOHN 4:32-34

DAY 331

A prayer about FRIENDSHIP
When I want to be more open to those I care about

HOLY SPIRIT,

I am so grateful for my friends. I'm afraid, however, that I am not always the kind of friend that I should be. Some of these relationships have drifted to the superficial. That is, my friends and I like each other and spend time together; but I don't share from my heart, and I am afraid to speak truth. At times I let petty disagreements over issues such as politics, favorite teams, or movies come between us. Friendship should transcend those differences, but I magnify them. I want to be a better friend. Jesus said that we should love each other, and his kind of love thinks of the other person first and not my own agenda or preferences. Friendship also involves confrontation—one person telling the other hard truths about morality, ethics, and other life choices. I confess that I have not been open to those conversations and have, rather, been defensive and irritated. Spirit, I want to change, to be the right kind of friend. Please continue to convict me of my callous indifference and pride. Help me to love.

[Jesus said,] "This is my commandment: Love each other in the same way I have loved you. There is no greater love than to lay down one's life for one's friends." JOHN 15:12-13

A prayer about GLORIFYING GOD
When I should praise the Lord

HEAVENLY FATHER,
You have said that your people should "do it all," *everything*, for your glory. I admit that I am usually concerned about *my* glory—getting the credit, the accolades—but I need to think about shining the spotlight on you, thanking you for any success I achieve. Also, like most people, I tend to divide life into sacred and secular and usually keep those worlds separate. I think I know how to glorify you in those "sacred" pursuits, such as worshiping, teaching Sunday school, leading youth group, praying, and reading the Bible. But those activities comprise just a small part of my life. What about the rest? I want to bring glory to your name at work—in how I relate to coworkers, my attitude and speech, and the way I do my job. I also want to bring glory to you in how I shop, interact socially, drive, and play. But glorifying you also means in every situation, even those painful, gut-wrenching, devastating experiences. I want to, Father. I want to live and die for your glory.

I will praise you, LORD, with all my heart; I will tell of all the marvelous things you have done. I will be filled with joy because of you. I will sing praises to your name, O Most High.
PSALM 9:1-2

DAY 332

A prayer about DEFENDING THE FAITH
When I encounter skeptics

ETERNAL FATHER,

My usual way of acting in an argument is to prove t other person wrong, hitting hard with facts and logi I want to *win*, probably because I'm so competitive bu also, I'll have to admit, because it bolsters my self-esteer and confidence. But at such times I'm really only thinkin of myself and not about the issue or the other individual. I'm especially vulnerable to this approach when someone says something outrageous about the Christian faith. And so I attack, hitting hard. That approach tends to win the debate but lose the person. And one place where I don't want that to happen is in someone's relationship with you, for that has eternal consequences. You have told me to be ready to explain my faith, Lord, and to do it in a gentle and respectful way. So please help me hold my tongue and respectfully listen to the other person's position. Then give me the words to say in those moments and the right attitude in saying them. And help my life match my words I want to be a positive representative of Christ.

You must worship Christ as Lord of your life. And if someone asks about your Christian hope, always be ready t explain it. But do this in a gentle and respectful way. Keep your conscience clear. Then if people speak against you, th will be ashamed when they see what a good life you live because you belong to Christ. 1 PETER 3:15-16

A prayer about FEAR
When I feel afraid

MY GREAT SHEPHERD,
I get so afraid, and I need you close, to find my hope and security in you. Fear hits suddenly, without warning, often totally unexpected. It can be numbing, debilitating, even paralyzing. Because of all the media options these days, I know much about what is going on around the world, and that gets to me, especially when the news at home and abroad seems terrible. I begin to feel as though the world is falling apart. Or a mysterious physical symptom blindsides me, and I think the worst. Another recurring fear relates to my financial security and the future. Little children often are afraid of storms or animals or monsters under the bed—immature and irrational to my older, informed way of thinking. But how must you see the source of *my* fears; they are nothing to you. At times, of course, I need to have a healthy fear. But in *every* situation I need to stay close to you, as a lamb to its Shepherd, protected and secure in your presence and following your lead.

Even when I walk through the darkest valley, I will not be afraid, for you are close beside me. Your rod and your staff protect and comfort me. PSALM 23:4

DAY 335 *Prayerful Moment*

A prayer about THE GOOD LIFE
When I become enamored of lifestyle enticements

GOD,
I have been tempted lately by stories of the rich and famous and all the attractive ads for entertainment, apparel, and other symbols of what most consider the good life. I know better; I know that all that is truly *good* comes from you. Help me keep my eyes, ears, mind, and priorities where they belong—glorifying you. That is the good life.

Don't be misled. . . . Whatever is good and perfect comes down to us from God our Father. JAMES 1:16-17

DAY 336 *Prayerful Moment*

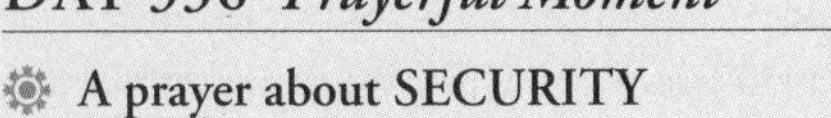

A prayer about SECURITY
When I must let go

GOD,
Toddlers with security blankets are cute, but adult versions are not. When Jesus told a potential follower to divest himself of his riches, the man couldn't do it, turning away from the Savior and life. Wealth was his idol, his security. Reveal my idol-blankets, Lord. Give me the strength to drop them at your feet. I want to depend on you alone.

[Jesus said,] "Go and sell all your possessions and give the money to the poor, and you will have treasure in heaven. Then come, follow me." At this the man's face fell, and he went away sad, for he had many possessions.
MARK 10:21-22

DAY 337

A prayer about REPENTANCE
When I need to turn around

DEAR LORD,

I remember seeing billboards and signs with one word, *Repent!* and thinking the message was quaint and out of touch with modern life. But here I am, needing to do just that. I am sinning, dear God, and I need to stop. I need forgiveness. I need you. I know that repentance literally means turning around and going in the opposite direction. This means stopping my move away from you. It also means regretting and rejecting that course of action and making a 180-degree turn. Jesus preached "repent and believe"—negative and positive, turn away from sin and go toward God. So right now I reject that sinful way of life and trust only in you. I believe, Lord, but please strengthen that belief and my faith. I move away from you and don't live your way because I have a sinful nature and because I am tempted on every side. But you made me new when I trusted Christ as Savior, so now, empowered by your Spirit, I can make God-honoring decisions and choices. Give me strength.

Repent of your sins and turn to God, so that your sins may be wiped away. ACTS 3:19

A prayer about BEING A CHRISTIAN
When I identify with Christ

MY SAVIOR,

I call myself a Christian. But to many that just means that I am not an atheist, a Jew, a Muslim, a Hindu, or something else. Ever since its founding, my nation has claimed to be "Christian," and most citizens would put that as religious preference on a poll. In my community, numerous institutions have that in their titles. But I know that, much more than a historical designation or religious category, the word means "Christ-one." So ostensibly Christians are claiming to be your devoted followers, identified with you. I think it also means that we should be like you. You told the disciples that they could see the Father by looking at you and that people should be able to see you in them. So, dear Jesus, as one who claims to be a Christian, I want to be worthy of that name, even as our society becomes increasingly unchristian. I promise, with your strength, to keep my focus on you and try to emulate your values, attitude, perspective, and actions. When people look at me, may they see you.

Barnabas went on to Tarsus to look for Saul. When he found him, he brought him back to Antioch. Both of them stayed there with the church for a full year, teaching large crowds of people. (It was at Antioch that the believers were first called Christians.) ACTS 11:25-26

A prayer about GOD'S MERCY

When I try to understand the depth of the Savior's love

MOST MERCIFUL LORD AND SAVIOR,

My sins were so great and vile. I had turned my back on you, failing to do what you wanted and not doing what you commanded—willfully rebelling against you. I was born a sinner, and I proved it by sinning continually. Depraved through and through, I had nothing good to offer you. I was totally and absolutely lost and condemned, deserving your displeasure and punishment. Hell was my sure destination. But in your infinite mercy, you didn't give me what I deserved—eternal death. And in your boundless grace, you gave me what I didn't deserve—eternal life. You, the perfect Lamb of God, died for me, in my place, taking *my* punishment. In your love you chose me, called me, and redeemed me. Now I stand forgiven, freed, justified, and bound for heaven. And I live each day by your continuous mercy and grace. I can only exclaim, "Thank you, Jesus!" How can I respond except to worship and praise you and live for you each day? I love you, Lord.

God is so rich in mercy, and he loved us so much, that even though we were dead because of our sins, he gave us life when he raised Christ from the dead. (It is only by God's grace that you have been saved!) EPHESIANS 2:4-5

DAY 340

A prayer about THE HOLY SPIRIT
When I begin to understand this member of the Trinity

HOLY SPIRIT,
Forgive me for overlooking you. The Trinity is such a mystery, but I know you are real and that Father, Son, and Holy Spirit are one. You are not a separate deity or part of God—you are fully God. Jesus told his disciples that after he left, he would send you. You are called "Advocate" because of your work highlighting the truth and pointing people to Jesus. You are also called "Comforter" because you come alongside your people. You have, indeed, come into the world and into me because I received you when I gave my life to Christ. You guide me into truth; you convict me of my sin; you produce fruit; you empower me to share the gospel with others; you change me when I allow you to do your powerful work in me. I know I grieve you when I ignore your leading and when I deliberately sin. Forgive me. I submit to you, Holy Spirit. Do what you want with me and release your power through me.

[Jesus said,] "It is best for you that I go away, because if I don't, the Advocate won't come. If I do go away, then I will send him to you. And when he comes, he will convict the world of its sin, and of God's righteousness, and of the coming judgment. . . . When the Spirit of truth comes, he will guide you into all truth. . . . He will tell you about the future. He will bring me glory by telling you whatever he receives from me." JOHN 16:7-8, 13-14

A prayer about LOVE
When I consider the depth of my affection

DEAR LORD,

At a wedding recently, I heard excerpts read from 1 Corinthians 13—the "love chapter." Weddings are all about love—songs, vows, and expressions of devotion. I first thought of love as a feeling. So as a child, the word described my deep affection, and my expressions were sincere and heartfelt. These days, grown-up love seems to be something one seeks, hopes for, and possesses—very self-oriented. But that seems to be even more immature than my childlike understanding, especially in light of Paul's profound description, which seems to highlight an attitude and a choice. And when I think of Jesus telling us to follow his example, I see that love involves action. I love when I choose to act in someone else's best interests, thinking about that person and not myself. O Lord, I am still so immature in my love. You loved me when I was living apart from you and against you. And it wasn't a warm, fuzzy feeling; you sent Jesus to *die* for me. You chose; you acted; you gave! Teach me to love.

If I could speak all the languages of earth and of angels, but didn't love others, I would only be a noisy gong or a clanging cymbal. . . . Three things will last forever—faith, hope, and love—and the greatest of these is love.

1 CORINTHIANS 13:1, 13

DAY 342 *Prayerful Moment*

A prayer about LOSS
When I evaluate my profit-and-loss statement

DEAR JESUS,

Many people measure success with a financial profit-and-loss statement. I know that you turn society's values upside down, and that a relationship with you is more valuable than anything the world rates as important. So whatever I have "lost" in culture's view is nothing. I have nothing without you. I want to know you, my Savior.

If you try to hang on to your life, you will lose it. But if you give up your life for my sake, you will save it. And what do you benefit if you gain the whole world but are yourself lost or destroyed? LUKE 9:24-25

DAY 343 *Prayerful Moment*

A prayer about LOYALTY
When I evaluate my relationships

HEAVENLY FATHER,

I am intensely loyal to those I love and will defend them against all sorts of attacks. I know, however, that loyalty can sometimes blind me to faults. So please temper my loyalty with openness and honesty. When sharing truth is necessary, help me be kind, speaking with love.

Never let loyalty and kindness leave you! Tie them around your neck as a reminder. Write them deep within your heart. Then you will find favor with both God and people, and you will earn a good reputation. PROVERBS 3:3-4

DAY 344

A prayer about EMPTINESS

When I feel completely drained

O SOVEREIGN LORD,

I began the week with energy, enthusiasm, and optimism, knowing what I had to accomplish and eager to get to it. But after a day or two, I feel exactly the opposite—downcast and defeated. I am wiped out, totally drained, and dry, as though I have nothing left to give. Every place I turn, I encounter many who continue to want more from me than I can give, and today I moved from one person and one crisis to the next—all day. This recent turn of events is affecting my attitude and outlook on life. By the time I got home, I had lost my appetite and motivation, and I tired doing even small tasks. I need spiritual nourishment, Lord—strength, endurance, patience, and hope, which can only come from you. I need a fresh touch of your Spirit. Fill my empty soul with joy, I pray. And please give me rest, with a good night's sleep, so I will awaken ready to face the responsibilities and challenges of a new day.

We also pray that you will be strengthened with all his glorious power so you will have all the endurance and patience you need. May you be filled with joy.

COLOSSIANS 1:11

DAY 345

A prayer about VOICES AND CHOICES
When I have spiritual options

HOLY SPIRIT,

This truly is the information age. Because of technology, every day I learn more about the world and life than I ever thought possible. Everyone seems to have a smart phone with a camera, so images and messages are broadcast continually. The assault on my senses includes many choices in every area of life, including lifestyles, morals, and religion. And it goes beyond awareness: these voices urge me to make decisions, to choose. I know what I believe; I am fully committed to Christ as my Savior and Lord—that's not up for debate. But I still wade through the other options. And persuasive spokespersons for distinct theological positions have been entering the scene through e-mails, broadcast media, and bestselling books. Some media personalities and people I know have been raving about them. So I ask you to help me sort through all of this as I compare their teachings to your inspired Word. Give me godly discernment, dear Holy Spirit. Lead me and strengthen me to reject the voices of error and choose only those options that honor you.

[Moses said,] "Today I have given you the choice between life and death, between blessings and curses. Now I call on heaven and earth to witness the choice you make. Oh, that you would choose life, so that you and your descendants might live!" DEUTERONOMY 30:19

DAY 346

A prayer about ATONEMENT
When I think about what Jesus did for me

MY SAVIOR,
I thought about the Cross today and what you experienced as a human being, a man. You humbled yourself completely to become a cluster of miniscule cells inside Mary and then a tiny baby. Born during difficult times in occupied territory, you submitted to parents and experienced childhood and adolescence, with all those human limitations. You lived perfectly, resisting every temptation. Then, enduring opposition from family, the religious establishment, and others, and after teaching and healing, you were falsely accused, hated, battered, bruised, whipped until bloody, mocked, spit upon, abandoned, tortured, and hung by through-the-flesh nails on those beams. But your greatest pain came as you became the sin bearer on that execution pole—the perfect and holy Son of God, the one who knew no sin becoming sin. Yet that was your choice. And you did it for me and all those who trust in you. You took the Cross in my place. Now I stand forgiven, Spirit indwelled, a child of God. Thank you, Jesus, for your love and sacrifice. I bow in humility, worshiping you, my Savior.

God showed how much he loved us by sending his one and only Son into the world so that we might have eternal life through him. This is real love—not that we loved God, but that he loved us and sent his Son as a sacrifice to take away our sins. 1 JOHN 4:9-10

DAY 347

A prayer about PRAYER
When I need to talk with my Father

HEAVENLY FATHER,

I rushed through today, moving from one responsibility and person to another, and I barely spoke with you. Forgive me. Because of Jesus' death and resurrection, I know that I can come directly into your presence at any time and in any place. I don't need the aid of another person or an animal sacrifice. The only barriers that ever stand between us have been erected by me because of my sin and neglect. Forgive me. You are the King of the universe, but you are my Father, and you have invited me to come boldly to your throne—what a profound privilege; yet I don't take advantage of it nearly enough. I get busy, but I should never be too busy to talk with you. Forgive me. Thank you for those sweet, extended times of prayer when I can pour out my deepest feelings, thoughts, and requests to you, and then just listen. And thank you for hearing my unspoken prayers and my thoughts directed to you, and for always being available to listen to my quick, whispered comments and requests. I love you, Lord.

Let us come boldly to the throne of our gracious God. There we will receive his mercy, and we will find grace to help us when we need it most. HEBREWS 4:16

A prayer about HARVEST
When I look on the mission fields

AWESOME LORD,
Jesus looked on the assembled crowds with compassion. I admit that if I had been one of the twelve disciples, I would have had a different take on the situation, probably seeing the people as an inconvenience, interruption, or threat to my access to the Master. Jesus saw them as lost souls who needed saving. That was his mission, why he came to earth. Since this incident, many have taken Jesus' words seriously and have worked tirelessly in the mission fields. In fact, if not for a faithful worker, I would still be lost in my sin. Today, the harvest is still great and the workers few. People are waiting to hear the gospel and respond, but they need someone to tell it to them. You have entrusted this task to your followers. So I pray for eyes of compassion and a willing heart. Even tonight, please bring individuals to mind for whom I should be praying. Then, beginning tomorrow morning, lead me to those with whom I can share Christ. I want to tell my story and introduce them to the Savior.

When [Jesus] saw the crowds, he had compassion on them because they were confused and helpless, like sheep without a shepherd. He said to his disciples, "The harvest is great, but the workers are few. So pray to the Lord who is in charge of the harvest; ask him to send more workers into his fields."
MATTHEW 9:36-38

DAY 349 *Prayerful Moment*

A prayer about DESTINY
When I consider my soul's ultimate destination

GRACIOUS LORD,
Today I was reminded of three profound truths: I know you; you are in control; you love me. Thus I can live confidently, believing that you control my destiny. So, knowing the future is settled, I am free to live for you. Job held that truth through terrible suffering and loss. My troubles are so small compared to his, but my hope is the same—living each day knowing that I belong to you.

He will do to me whatever he has planned. He controls my destiny. JOB 23:14

DAY 350 *Prayerful Moment*

A prayer about URGENCY
When I realize that time is running out

FATHER,
"Christ could return at any moment!" I have heard that for years, and I know it's true. But the implied urgency fades as time goes by. Paul told first-century believers that time was running out—how much more so now! Every day brings us closer to the end, one less day for people to repent and believe. Wake me from my complacency. Lead me to those with whom I can share Jesus' story and love.

This is all the more urgent, for you know how late it is; time is running out. Wake up, for our salvation is nearer now than when we first believed. ROMANS 13:11

DAY 351

A prayer about the TEMPLE OF THE HOLY SPIRIT

When I recognize God's holy presence in all believers

HOLY SPIRIT,

Every person I meet bears the image of the Creator. You value all of them, so I should treat them with respect and honor. And every person who has trusted Christ as Savior is your child, my brother or sister in the faith. You live in each of us individually and corporately—we are your temple. I read harsh words in 1 and 2 Corinthians about what happens to those who would destroy this place. I admit that I have come close, with feelings of animosity toward certain Christian family members. I haven't acted on those feelings, but I have been mentally composing nasty letters and cutting comments. Forgive me, Lord. I love the church, but loving individual members is often quite difficult. So please work on my attitude, emotions, and mind, I pray. I am quick to forgive myself when I do what others don't appreciate—I have excuses at the ready. So why don't I give others the same benefit of the doubt? Help me glorify you by loving them, as all together we are your temple.

Don't you realize that all of you together are the temple of God and that the Spirit of God lives in you? God will destroy anyone who destroys this temple. For God's temple is holy, and you are that temple. 1 CORINTHIANS 3:16-17

DAY 352

A prayer about BROKENNESS

When I realize the full extent of my sinfulness

GENTLE HEALER,

I need you . . . desperately. I want to do what is right, to live for you, but I keep falling back into sin. And I gave in to temptation and fell today into those sinful patterns, despite having pledged never to do so again. I feel as though I have let you down. I am ashamed, broken, and desperate. I can identify with Paul in his struggle with the sinful nature. Even when I do what is good, my motives are bad—shallow, self-centered, ego driven. Forgive me, cleanse me, heal me, restore me, draw me close, dear Lord. Please show me what I need to do to make amends with those I have wronged, against whom I have sinned. And give me the resolve, courage, and strength to move forward, sinful but forgiven. I want to be your person in this world, but this was not a good day. Thank you for loving and forgiving me, for your mercy and grace.

I have discovered this principle of life—that when I want to do what is right, I inevitably do what is wrong. I love God's law with all my heart. But there is another power within me that is at war with my mind. This power makes me a slave to the sin that is still within me. Oh, what a miserable person I am! Who will free me from this life that is dominated by sin and death? Thank God! The answer is in Jesus Christ our Lord. ROMANS 7:21-25

A prayer about GOD'S PROMISES
When I am reassured by the Word

GOD,

As I peruse and study your Word, I am almost overwhelmed with joy as I read your promises to your people. Every sentence of these affirmative statements exudes your love and care. Peter calls these "great and precious promises." You are perfect, true, and good and can do anything you say you will because of your knowledge and power. Nothing can ever compare with the gifts you give to those you love. You have promised to be our Father, adopting us as your children, and to send the Holy Spirit to live in us. You have promised to always be with us, everywhere and in every circumstance. You have promised peace, power, healing, security, comfort, deliverance, hope, encouragement, joy, guidance, rest, strength, endurance, confidence, and so much more. And the greatest gift and promise of all: eternal life through Christ. I know beyond any doubt that eventually you will take me home, and I will live forever with you. Hallelujah!

By his divine power, God has given us everything we need for living a godly life. We have received all of this by coming to know him, the one who called us to himself by means of his marvelous glory and excellence. And because of his glory and excellence, he has given us great and precious promises. These are the promises that enable you to share his divine nature and escape the world's corruption caused by human desires.

2 PETER 1:3-4

DAY 354

A prayer about DISCOURAGEMENT
When my losses pile up

JESUS,

No doubt about it—I am living and moving in a rut, following the unchanging route and routine with no end in sight. I seem to fight the same battles day after day without very much progress. Victories, small and few, are seldom won. So I continue to slog through the daily schedule, doing my best to meet my responsibilities, but it is tough. And lately this struggle has got me down and has been affecting my relationships—I confess that I am not too much fun to be around. I feel beaten, alone, and discouraged. I remember as a child joyfully anticipating a grand celebration, a family vacation, an extended visit from a beloved relative, summer camp, or a special event at church. These days, I feel as though I have nothing to look forward to, just another day of the same old same old. Please lift my spirits, Savior. I cling to the knowledge that you go ahead of me and are with me. Give me your hope and joy, I pray. I want to sing again.

Why am I discouraged? Why is my heart so sad? I will put my hope in God! I will praise him again—my Savior and my God! PSALM 43:5

A prayer about GRACE

When I consider God's kindness toward me

MOST GRACIOUS HEAVENLY FATHER,
I am beginning to get a glimpse of what motivated John Newton to write the words to his classic hymn, "Amazing Grace." I have often sung that song and have affirmed for years that salvation is by grace alone and that I don't deserve your favor. But when I consider the depths of my depravity—my sinful nature, willful acts of disobedience, neglect of spending time with you, thoughts that constantly violate your commands and desires, lack of faith, and an almost eagerness to go my own way—I can scarcely believe that you pay any attention to me at all, let alone that you love and forgive me. I know that Jesus died for all who believe, throughout the whole world and the millennia—millions and millions of people. But he died for *me*, paying the penalty for *my* sin on the cross. I can never repay your kindness toward me, of course—but you don't want me to try. You just want my heart. In humble surrender, I worship you, Lord. What profound and amazing grace!

We believe that we are all saved the same way, by the undeserved grace of the Lord Jesus. ACTS 15:11

DAY 356 *Prayerful Moment*

A prayer about COMFORT
When I am grieving

PRECIOUS HOLY SPIRIT,
Sorrow consumes; grief overwhelms. Every minute today has been a struggle as I remember and consider the loss of one I held so dear. I feel empty and alone. I know the truth—that life is short and eternity awaits—but I hurt so much. Divine Comforter, right now I need you—desperately. Please wipe my tears. Hold me close. Help me get through this night and tomorrow. Give me hope.

Let your unfailing love comfort me, just as you promised me, your servant. PSALM 119:76

DAY 357 *Prayerful Moment*

A prayer about GOSSIP
When I pass on a rumor

GRACIOUS GOD,
After taking part in a discussion recently, I wondered why I had said anything at all and especially why I had passed on what I had heard about the person in question. That's gossip, plain and simple, and it is sin. I probably wanted to be accepted by the group or to feel as though I had inside information. Please forgive me, Lord. And in the future, help me to think before I speak and to refuse to gossip and spread rumors.

Do not spread slanderous gossip among your people.
LEVITICUS 19:16

A prayer about COUNTING THE COST
When I pledge to follow Christ

ETERNAL GOD,

Large crowds followed Jesus, listening to him teach and watching him perform miracles. He had celebrity status. So Jesus spoke to them about counting the cost of following him, including carrying a "cross." The people knew the full meaning of carrying a cross—it wasn't a metaphor to them, because they had seen it almost daily. Even so, they didn't understand the full extent of the persecution they would encounter. Still today, throughout the world, courageous men and women are being tortured and martyred for following the Savior. I face nothing like that, my God, so I can easily pledge my total allegiance to you and the gospel. And often I speak boldly of being your disciple. But talk is cheap, Lord. Help me count the cost and be willing to pay the price. This may include harsh criticism and ridicule, broken relationships, and perhaps even physical persecution. But I want to be your person—at all times, everywhere, no matter what. Please help me.

If you do not carry your own cross and follow me, you cannot be my disciple. But don't begin until you count the cost. For who would begin construction of a building without first calculating the cost to see if there is enough money to finish it? Otherwise, you might complete only the foundation before running out of money, and then everyone would laugh at you. They would say, "There's the person who started that building and couldn't afford to finish it!" LUKE 14:27-30

A prayer about WATCHING AND WAITING

When I see the signs of the times

DEAR JESUS,

You have promised to return, and you keep all your promises. You told your disciples about the events preceding the Second Coming. These signs include a spike in wars, natural disasters, and intense maltreatment of believers. As I hear the news reports and read the accounts of the persecuted church, I believe I am witnessing the predictions being fulfilled. You also said that when those events occur, your followers should get ready because your return would be soon. Some think this means they should stop everything and just wait somewhere for you. I know you don't want that; instead, I should be alert, prepared, and expectant because you could return at any moment, even tonight. So as I am watching and waiting, I need to be a responsible member of my family, church, and community, serving others and living for you. I praise you, Lord Jesus, for your first coming, during which you died on the cross for me. And I praise you for your second one, yet to come.

There will be strange signs in the sun, moon, and stars. And here on earth the nations will be in turmoil, perplexed by the roaring seas and strange tides. People will be terrified at what they see coming upon the earth, for the powers in the heavens will be shaken. Then everyone will see the Son of Man coming on a cloud with power and great glory. So when all these things begin to happen, stand and look up, for your salvation is near! LUKE 21:25-28

A prayer about CRISIS

When my peace is suddenly interrupted

DEAR GOD,

Awakening, preparing for my day, and then moving through it with my usual duties and responsibilities, I thought I had a pretty good idea of what would happen next, especially since everything seemed normal, fine, calm, and routine. Then suddenly I was blindsided—the phone call and subsequent e-mails out of nowhere, with news I never expected and certainly didn't want. I was turned upside down—a promising day turned into disaster. I was confused, hurting, and left to do damage control. My feelings fluctuated between anguish and anger, and my next steps seemed unclear and unsteady. I feel like David, Lord, "alone and in deep distress." And I, too, plead for your rescue and refuge. First, I desperately need your peace in the moment—calm my spirit and assure me of your presence. I also need your direction and guidance for my next decision and response. What should I do next? Who can I enlist to help? And I need hope for the future. Please, Lord, I need to get through this—with you—and to honor you in the process.

Turn to me and have mercy, for I am alone and in deep distress. My problems go from bad to worse. Oh, save me from them all! Feel my pain and see my trouble. . . . Protect me! Rescue my life from them! Do not let me be disgraced, for in you I take refuge. May integrity and honesty protect me, for I put my hope in you. PSALM 25:16-18, 20-21

A prayer about RETALIATION
When I want to get even

HOLY SPIRIT,

I am furious. I was wronged and want to get even, to make the person who hurt me pay dearly. I need your help. Scripture makes very clear that retaliation is wrong—we shouldn't look for payback and return evil for evil, and we should leave revenge to you. But I'm having trouble letting go of these feelings. In fact, I fear what I might do if given the opportunity. In the grand scheme, the offense is not a big deal (I've heard of people who have even forgiven the murderer of a loved one), but I feel frustrated, betrayed, and angry. Do your work in me, I pray. Please change my attitude and feelings. Jesus said we should pray for our enemies, so that is where I will begin. This is tough, but right now I pray for ________. Please work in that life too. I also pray for reconciliation, that one day the offender and I might even be friends again. That would be a miracle, and I'm trusting you for it.

Never pay back evil with more evil. Do things in such a way that everyone can see you are honorable. Do all that you can to live in peace with everyone. Dear friends, never take revenge. Leave that to the righteous anger of God. For the Scriptures say, "I will take revenge; I will pay them back," says the LORD. . . . Don't let evil conquer you, but conquer evil by doing good. ROMANS 12:17-19, 21

A prayer about the NAMES OF GOD
When I study God's titles

JEHOVAH,

I am not a number or a letter. I am a person with a name. Before I was born, my parents considered many options for what to call me. Family history, special friends, unique meanings, and other factors informed the decision. And I have carried that moniker since birth—my first, middle, and last names. You know the power of a name, and you changed a few significant ones recorded in Scripture: Abram to Abraham, Sarai to Sarah, Jacob to Israel, Simon to Cephas or Peter, and more. The Bible also reveals your many titles, each one highlighting a profound aspect of your nature. I submit to you, Adonai-Jehovah—"The Lord our Sovereign"; El-Shaddai—"God Almighty"; Jehovah-Elohim—"The Eternal Creator"; El-Olam—"The Everlasting God"; Jehovah-Jireh—"The Lord our Provider." And I praise you as the great "I AM"— the one who is eternally existing, Alpha and Omega, beginning and end. I worship and adore you, my Lord and my God. What an amazing privilege to be your child and to serve you!

God replied to Moses, "I AM WHO I AM. Say this to the people of Israel: I AM has sent me to you." God also said to Moses, "Say this to the people of Israel: Yahweh, the God of your ancestors—the God of Abraham, the God of Isaac, and the God of Jacob—has sent me to you. This is my eternal name, my name to remember for all generations."
EXODUS 3:14-15

DAY 363 *Prayerful Moment*

A prayer about SLEEPING WELL
When I need a restful night

DEAR LORD,
I'm tired. It's been a long, tough day, and I need a good night's sleep, especially considering what's on the schedule for tomorrow. Help me to relax and rest in you, Father, secure in the knowledge that you are watching over me. Keep me from sleep-depriving concerns, worries, and other negative thoughts. Help me focus my thoughts on your goodness and the joy and hope you give me.

You will keep in perfect peace all who trust in you, all whose thoughts are fixed on you! ISAIAH 26:3

DAY 364 *Prayerful Moment*

A prayer about GOODNESS
When I truly understand God's nature

LORD,
I know the musical refrain, "God is good all the time." That's easy to sing and believe when I'm feeling fine, have money in the bank, and the future looks bright. But you are good *all the time*—even when I can't see you and life seems to be falling apart, or in the in-between times of gray ordinary. I know the truth, dear Father. And I hold on to it right now. Help me to trust you fully and to live joyfully, knowing that you are indeed good.

How kind the LORD is! How good he is! So merciful, this God of ours! PSALM 116:5

DAY 365

A prayer about HOME
When I yearn for the end of the journey

HEAVENLY FATHER,
I revel in being your child. Words cannot express the joy I feel knowing that I am yours, in your family. You have given me eternal life, filled me with your Spirit, and marked out my path, guiding every step of the way. Knowing that this life is not the end but just the beginning has filled me with hope as I look beyond. Regardless of how many days I have left in this world, you have prepared a place for me in the next. O Lord, I want to be a faithful follower, doing your will, serving others, and sharing the Good News about Christ, but I long for the moment I will be translated into your presence. I remember as a child being by myself away from my house. Though not far away, I felt lonely and lost. But then I was found and brought home—a joyous reunion. That's how I feel now, at the edge of heaven. I want to burst through the door and into your waiting arms to live in your house forever.

Surely your goodness and unfailing love will pursue me all the days of my life, and I will live in the house of the LORD forever. PSALM 23:6

TOPICAL INDEX

Abilities | Day 257
Adoption | Day 193
Affirmation | Day 212
Amen | Day 189
Anger | Day 299
Answers to Prayer | Day 256
Anxiety | Day 284
Appearance | Day 4
Applying Scripture | Day 259
Arguing | Day 195
Assurance | Day 22
Atonement | Day 346
Balance | Day 17
Beauty | Day 150
Being a Christian | Day 338
Being Known | Day 1
Being Spirit Led | Day 137
Being the Best | Day 317
Bible | Day 290
Blessings | Day 135
Body, My | Day 130
Body of Christ | Day 187
Brevity of Life | Day 319
Brokenness | Day 352
Burnout | Day 216
Busyness | Day 105
Caring for Others | Day 7
Change | Day 280
Character | Day 287
Cheating | Day 307
Childlike Faith | Day 214
Children | Day 19
Choices | Day 258
Chosen by God | Day 276
Church | Day 169
Clean Heart, A | Day 21
Comfort | Day 356
Commitment | Day 293
Communication | Day 92
Comparisons | Day 96
Compassion | Day 106
Competition | Day 203
Complacency | Day 302
Complaining | Day 304
Confidence | Day 133
Conflict | Day 226
Confrontation | Day 126
Conscience | Day 322
Contentment | Day 234
Controlling the Tongue | Day 78
Correction | Day 248
Counting the Cost | Day 358
Courage | Day 82
Coworkers | Day 186
Creation | Day 208
Crisis | Day 360
Critical Spirit | Day 38
Criticism | Day 321
Culture Wars | Day 241
Death | Day 5
Decisions | Day 27
Defeat | Day 116
Defending the Faith | Days 278, 332
Delay | Day 37
Depression | Day 272
Desires | Day 188
Destination | Day 16
Destiny | Day 349
Direction | Day 201
Disagreements | Day 110
Disappointment | Day 141
Discernment | Day 113
Discipline | Day 28
Discouragement | Day 354
Distractions | Day 288
Doubts | Day 145
Dreams and Nightmares | Day 99
Education | Day 152
Ego | Day 58
Emotions | Day 60
Empathy | Day 233
Emptiness | Day 344
Encouragement | Day 209
Enemies | Day 224
Energy | Day 121
Enjoying God | Day 231
Environment | Day 155
Envy | Day 98
Escape | Day 72
Eternal Life | Day 66
Eternity | Day 213
Everyday Miracles | Day 30
Everything New | Day 103
Evidence | Day 90
Example | Day 260
Excellence | Day 228
Exhaustion | Days 91, 206
Expectations | Day 93
Facing "Giants" | Day 327
Failure | Day 308
Faith | Day 285
Faith and Works | Day 142
Family | Day 170
Fear | Day 334
Fearfully and Wonderfully Made | Day 229
Finishing Strong | Day 227
Focus | Day 159
Following Jesus Daily | Day 11
Forgiveness | Day 301
Forgiving Others | Day 108
Fortitude | Day 33
Freedom | Day 204
Friends | Day 255
Friendship | Day 331
Fun | Day 305
Future Dreams | Day 153

Future Fears | Day 9
Generosity | Day 88
Giving | Day 194
Glorifying God | Days 40, 333
Goals | Day 157
God Moments | Day 247
God's Call | Day 179
God's Care | Day 112
God's Image | Day 144
God's Mercy | Day 339
God's Presence | Day 183
God's Promises | Day 353
God's Support | Day 23
God's Will | Day 165
Going the Distance | Day 124
Good Life, The | Day 335
Goodness | Day 364
Gossip | Day 357
Government | Day 81
Grace | Day 355
Gratitude | Day 312
Grief | Day 143
Growth | Day 77
Guidance | Day 175
Guilt | Day 131
Habits | Day 184
Happiness | Day 53
Hard Work | Day 177
Harvest | Day 348
Healing | Day 87
Health | Day 107
Heart Troubles | Day 55
Heaven | Day 44
Help | Day 41
Holiness | Day 54
Holy Spirit, The | Day 340
Home | Day 365
Honesty | Day 191
Hope | Day 6
Humility | Day 230
Hurts | Day 70
Hypocrisy | Day 138
Illumination | Day 39
Image of God | Day 292
Incarnation, The | Day 172
Influence | Day 281
Insecurity | Day 42
Inspiration | Day 109
Integrity | Day 222
Irritations | Day 309
Jealousy | Day 3
Jesus | Days 71, 97
Joy | Day 29
Judging Others | Day 279
Keeping Promises | Day 52
Kindness | Day 48
King Jesus | Day 97
Knowing | Day 123
Knowing Christ | Day 50
Known by God | Day 1
Lasting | Day 104
Legacy | Day 20
Legalism | Day 211
Letting Go | Day 254
Life | Day 207
Life Lessons | Day 311
Light | Day 32
Limitations | Day 118
Listening to God | Day 146
Listening to Others | Day 74
Living for God | Day 101
Living One Day at a Time | Day 11
Living Sacrifice | Day 264
Loneliness | Day 173
Longings | Day 134
Loosening My Grip | Day 61
Lordship | Day 119
Loss | Day 342
Lost and Found | Day 270
Love | Day 341
Love for Believers | Day 200
Love for Enemies | Day 43
Love for God | Day 289
Loyalty | Day 343
Lust | Day 147
Making a Difference | Day 156
Making a Good Impression | Day 178
Making Ends Meet | Day 192
Making Progress | Day 79
Margin | Day 244
Materialism | Day 122
Maturity | Day 62
Meeting My Needs | Day 45
Meeting the Challenge | Day 8
Memories | Day 236
Mentoring | Day 67
Mercy toward Others | Day 36
Modeling Values | Day 63
Money | Day 238
Morality | Day 176
Motives | Day 114
Names of God, The | Day 362
Narrow Way, The | Day 324
Necessities | Day 291
Needs | Day 12
Neighbors | Day 161
New Creation | Day 160
New Life | Day 252
Obedience | Day 95
Obstacles | Day 31
Opportunities | Day 129
Opposition | Day 267
Organization | Day 132
Overcoming | Day 303
Pain | Day 120
Passion | Day 94
Patience | Day 205
Paying It Forward | Day 325
Peace | Day 102
Peacemaking | Day 237
Perfection | Day 76
Persecuted Church, The | Day 149
Persecution | Day 15
Perseverance | Day 167